My Fast Metabolism Diet CookBook

The Wheat-Free, Soy-Free, Dairy-Free,
Corn-Free and Sugar-Free Cookbook

100 Delicious
Fast Metabolism Diet Friendly
Recipes That Your Family Will Love!

by

New Health CookBooks

ISBN: 1490928081
ISBN-13: 978-1490928081

COPYRIGHT

DISCLAIMER

New Health CookBooks

Contents

Contents

Contents

Contents

Contents

Introduction

The main purpose of The Fast Metabolism Diet by Haylie Pomroy is to jump-start your metabolism, which as the author states, in most people, is bogged down and working much slower than it should due to a typical diet high in sugars, refined carbs, and several other foods.

Some of the recipes in this cookbook are higher in portion size and total calorie counts than specifically recommended in the Fast Metabolism Diet book. Some people feel they need this option to be able to stay on the program, and many people are cooking for their loved ones also.

Make sure to follow the guidelines in the diet, and use good common sense when it comes to portion control and remember that you can always put some leftovers in the fridge for tomorrow.

Important note:

ALL ingredient options should be organic, wild-caught, grass-fed, responsibly farmed/raised/grown whenever possible.

These foods need to be **avoided** on this diet: Wheat, corn, dairy, soy, refined sugar, caffeine, fruit juices, and artificial sweeteners (except those specified)

Enjoy!

New Health CookBooks

Chapter 1

Phase 1

High Glycemic, Moderate Protein, Low Fat Meals

Phase One Breakfasts

Raspberry-Pumpkin Oatmeal

With the homey and comforting flavors of pumpkin pie plus the tart, refreshing tang of raspberries, this Phase 1 breakfast comes together quickly. Frozen raspberries may be substituted; thaw before using.

Serves: 1

Ingredients

- ½ cup steel-cut oats
- ½ cup brown rice milk, unsweetened
- ½ teaspoon ground cinnamon
- ¼ cup pumpkin puree
- Ground cloves and nutmeg, to taste
- ¼ cup fresh raspberries

Preparation

In a small saucepan over medium high heat, combine oats, rice milk and cinnamon. Bring to a boil and cook, stirring continuously, until thick and creamy. Reduce heat to medium low; stir in additional spices and pumpkin and heat through. Serve hot, topped with raspberries.

Peach-Blueberry Smoothie

Perfect for rushed and hurried mornings, this surprisingly creamy smoothie packs your fruit and grain servings into one refreshing, frosty drink!

Serves: 1

Ingredients

- ¾ cup frozen cubed peaches
- ¼ cup frozen blueberries
- ½ cup unsweetened rice milk

Preparation

Combine the blueberries and peaches in a blender; add ¼ cup rice milk. Blend until smooth; add remaining rice milk, if necessary, to reach desired consistency.

Loganberry French Toast

You'll never miss the traditional whole eggs or milk in this luscious and comforting French toast — loganberries provide an unexpected flavor twist, but feel free to substitute strawberries, blackberries, blueberries, mulberries or raspberries.

Serves: 1

Ingredients

- 1 thick slice sprouted-grain bread
- 1 egg white
- ⅛ teaspoon ground cinnamon
- ⅛ teaspoon ground nutmeg
- ¼ teaspoon vanilla extract
- ½ cup fresh or frozen loganberries
- 1 tablespoon fresh lemon juice

Preparation

Heat a skillet or griddle over medium-high heat. In a small bowl, whisk egg white, cinnamon, nutmeg and vanilla. Dip the bread into egg mixture, coating both sides evenly. Cook until crisp and golden brown on both sides.

In a small saucepan, combine berries and lemon juice; cook over medium heat until berries are soft. Immediately spoon over French toast slice and serve.

Refreshing Fruit Salad

Forget the refined-sugar dressings featured in most fruit salad recipes —
this brightly flavored breakfast option relies on natural sweetness.

Serves: 4

Ingredients

- 1¼ cups chopped watermelon
- 1 small orange, sectioned and peeled
- 10 large strawberries, trimmed and halved or chopped
- 1 apple, cored, seeded and chopped
- 1 peach, peeled and sliced
- 1 apricot, sliced
- 15 sweet cherries, pitted and sliced
- ¼ cup blueberries
- 1 lime
- Fresh mint leaves, chopped
- ½ teaspoon Stevia (optional)

Preparation

In a bowl, combine all fruits. Halve and juice the lime; add to fruit mixture to taste. Add the mint and Stevia (if desired) to taste.

Serve alongside a toasted sprouted-grain bagel.

Baked Pie-Spiced Apples

For a relaxing weekend brunch option, these delicious baked apples have all the flavors of an apple pie without the refined carbs of traditional crusts! Choose baking apples, as they can be cooked without becoming mushy.

Serves: 4

Ingredients

- ¾ cup prepared steel-cut oats (made with unsweetened rice milk)
- 4 large baking apples, cored
- 1 teaspoon cinnamon
- ¼ teaspoon ground nutmeg
- 1 tablespoon (or more to taste) grated fresh ginger)
- ¾ cup boiling water.

Preparation

Preheat oven to 375. Place washed and cored apples in an eight-inch square baking pan. Stuff each apple with oatmeal; sprinkle with spices and ginger. Pour the boiling water into the pan. Bake for 30 to 40 minutes or until desired tenderness is reached; paste with pan drippings and serve immediately.

Exotic Fruit Salad

With its unexpected blend of zippy flavors, this unique fruit salad is great for days when you crave something a little bit different! Serve alongside a toasted sprouted-grain bagel to complete your Phase One breakfast.

Serves: 6

Ingredients

- 1 small, fresh pineapple, peeled and chopped
- 2 papayas, peeled and chopped
- 2 mangoes, peeled and chopped
- ⅓ cup rice vinegar
- ⅛ teaspoon nutmeg
- 1 tablespoon grated fresh ginger
- 2 kiwis, peeled and chopped
- 1 cup strawberries, trimmed and sliced
- 2 tablespoons fresh mint, chopped

Preparation

In a blender, combine ½ cup pineapple, 1 cup papaya and 1 cup mango. Add the vinegar, nutmeg and ginger; blend until pureed and smooth.

Combine remaining ingredients in a serving bowl; add enough dressing to coat and serve immediately.

Toasty Brown Rice Cereal

Not just for babies anymore, this hearty and satisfying brown rice cereal is an ideal oatmeal alternative for cold mornings when you want something to warm you up!

Serves: 1 (several servings can be made from one batch of toasted rice)

Ingredients

- 4 cups brown rice
- Additions: fresh berries or any Phase 1 acceptable fruits; cinnamon; ginger; nutmeg

Preparation

Heat a large cast-iron skillet over medium heat. Add the rice and toast, stirring constantly, approximately 10 minutes or until light-to-medium brown in color. If your rice begins to burn, turn heat down immediately.

In a food processor, working in ¾ cup batches, process the slightly cooled rice until it reaches the consistency of medium-grain cornmeal. Do not over-process into a powder.

Store in an airtight container in your refrigerator or freezer; this cereal will go rancid at room temperature.

To Prepare:

In a saucepan, boil 1 cup water. Add ⅓ cup brown rice cereal and stir for approximately thirty seconds. Reduce heat to a simmer; cover and cook approximately ten minutes until desired consistency is reached.

Top using fruit and spices.

Bowl-of-Cherries Stuffed Cantaloupe

Loaded with sweet fruit taste and ultra-simple to create, this cheerful breakfast is great when you need something quick but still special. Serve alongside a toasted sprouted-grain bagel or thick slice of toasted sprouted-grain bread to complete your Phase One breakfast.

Serves: 1

Ingredients

- ½ of a fresh, ripe cantaloupe
- ¾ cup sweet cherries, pitted
- ½ fresh lime
- ⅛ teaspoon Stevia (optional)
- Torn fresh mint leaves

Preparation

Using a melon baller or spoon, scoop out the cantaloupe flesh, leaving a ½ inch ring. Coarsely chop the melon and combine with the cherries and mint; juice the lime over the fruit and toss to coat. Serve in melon half; sprinkle with Stevia if desired.

Roasted Spiced Pears

Elegant and delicious, this simple breakfast option brings out the delicate flavors of pears in a whole new way! Oatmeal completes this hearty Phase One breakfast option.

Serves: 4

Ingredients

- 1 ½ pounds Bosc pears, slightly under-ripe, peeled and cored
- 2 to 3 tablespoons water
- 2 tablespoons freshly squeezed lemon juice
- ¼ teaspoon vanilla extract
- 1 teaspoon ground cinnamon
- ¼ teaspoon ground nutmeg

Preparation

Preheat oven to 375 degrees and arrange the pears, cut-side-up, on a rimmed baking sheet. Pour the water into the baking sheet. Combine the lemon juice and vanilla; drizzle over pears. Bake for 35 minutes to one hour, depending on size of pears, until soft but not mushy.

Sprinkle with cinnamon and nutmeg; serve immediately alongside or in a serving of steel-cut oatmeal.

Strawberry-Pomegranate Oatmeal

Simple, familiar and satisfying, this quick recipe adds a little something new by incorporating juice-filled pomegranate seeds!

Serves: 1

Ingredients

- ¼ cup steel-cut oats
- ¾ cup water
- 2 tablespoons unsweetened rice milk
- ½ cup fresh or frozen (thawed) strawberries
- 1 pomegranate, seeds removed and saved
- ¼ teaspoon cinnamon (optional)

Preparation

In a small saucepan, combine oats, water and rice milk. Bring to a boil; reduce heat and cook on low, uncovered, for 20 to 30 minutes, checking after 10 minutes for doneness and dryness. If the oats are drying out too quickly, add more water.

In a small bowl (or directly in oatmeal), combine strawberries and pomegranate seeds. Sprinkle with cinnamon if desired.

Phase One Lunches

Garden Fresh Chicken Sandwiches

Bursting with fresh flavor, these quick little sandwiches are perfect for packed lunches – the juicy crunch of fresh vegetables and spicy kick of mustard ensure you'll never miss the fat! To complete your Phase One lunch, be sure to enjoy these with a piece of fruit.

Serves: 4

Ingredients

- 4 sprouted-grain bagels OR 8 slices sprouted-grain bread
- 4 teaspoons prepared mustard
- 8 slices deli chicken, nitrate-free
- 8 slices tomato
- 16 slices cucumber

Preparation

Spread one side of each bagel OR 4 slices of bread with 1 teaspoon mustard. Stack sandwiches onto prepared slices; top with remaining slice or side. Serve immediately.

Sweet Turkey Sandwiches

With their unexpected flavor combination and easy preparation, these unique treats pack all your Phase One lunch components into a single sandwich! You could turn these sandwiches into wraps by substituting a sprouted-grain or spelt tortilla for the bread.

Serves: 4

Ingredients

- 8 slices thick sprouted-grain bread
- ⅓ cup prepared mustard, traditional or spicy brown
- 4 small (4 ounce) white meat turkey cutlets
- 2 small pears (such as Bosc), cored and sliced
- 2 cups lightly packed baby spinach, washed and patted dry
- 2 cups lightly packed arugula, washed and patted dry

Preparation

Brush the turkey cutlets with 3 tablespoons of mustard. In a nonstick skillet over medium heat, cook the cutlets for 2 to 3 minutes. Flip and cook another 2 to 3 minutes or until cooked through and no longer pink (170 degrees). Place 2 pears slices atop each cutlet. Cover skillet and remove from heat; let stand until pear slices are slightly softened.

Meanwhile, spread the remaining mustard on 4 slices of bread. Top each prepared slice with 1 cup greens and a pear-topped turkey cutlet.

Simple Chicken Salad with Strawberries

Fresh yet satisfying, this salad marries two classic favorites into one delicious Phase One lunch option!

Serves: 4

Ingredients

- 2 cups sliced fresh strawberries, trimmed, divided
- 1 pound chicken breasts, boneless, skinless
- 8 cups baby spinach leaves, washed and patted dry
- 2 tablespoons balsamic vinegar
- 4 sprouted-grain dinner rolls

Preparation

In a deep skillet over medium heat, cover chicken breasts with water and poach until cooked through and no pink remains (170 degrees). Remove from water, slice or shred, set aside.

In the meantime, place 1 cup strawberries in a food processor and process until smooth.

Divide spinach between four plates. Top with shredded chicken and remaining cup sliced strawberries. Drizzle with strawberry puree, then with balsamic vinegar.

Serve immediately with rolls.

Southwest Grilled Chicken Wraps

Zippy, southwest flavors make these grilled sandwiches a surefire healthy hit at your next cookout! Serve alongside a simple, sugar-free fruit salad to complete your Phase One lunch.

Serves: 4

Ingredients

- 4 tablespoons Simply Organic taco seasoning mix
- 4 chicken breasts, boneless, skinless
- 4 spelt or sprouted-grain tortillas
- 2 cups baby spinach, washed and patted dry
- 2 cups arugula, washed and patted dry
- ½ cup (or more to taste) salsa

Preparation

Prepare or set your grill to medium heat. Rub the chicken breasts with taco seasoning; wrap each in an aluminum foil packet, leaving room for steam to circulate.

Place packets over medium heat or coals. Cook for approximately 10 to 12 minutes, turning once, until chicken is cooked through and no longer pink (170 degrees). Set aside.

During the last few minutes of grilling, place tortillas on the grill to heat and char them slightly.

Assemble wraps by spreading approximately 1 tablespoon (add more or less to suit individual tastes) on half of each tortilla. Top with 1 cup mixed greens and a seasoned chicken breast; roll up and serve immediately.

Full-Bodied White Bean Soup

Packed with satisfying ingredients and with a surprisingly creamy texture thanks to mashed beans, this hearty soup is sure to please! Pair with an apple, pear or approved fruit of your choice and serve with toasted sprouted-grain rolls to round out your Phase One lunch.

Serves: 4

Ingredients

- 2 cans (15 ounces each) Great Northern beans, rinsed and drained, separated
- 1 cup chopped carrots
- 1 cup sliced celery
- ¼ cup chopped red onion
- 2 cloves fresh garlic, minced
- 3 cups plus 2 tablespoons chicken broth, homemade or canned (no artificial ingredients)
- 3 tablespoons chopped fresh basil leaves
- 2 teaspoons Simply Organic Italian seasoning blend
- ¼ teaspoon pepper (if desired)
- 4 cups baby spinach, washed and patted dry

Preparation

In a small bowl or a food processor, puree or mash ½ cup of beans until creamy. Set aside.

In a large nonstick saucepan over medium high heat, stirring often, sauté carrot, celery, onion and garlic in 2 tablespoons broth until vegetables are crisp but tender, approximately 3 to 4 minutes.

Add the remaining broth, beans and seasonings to saucepan. Bring to a boil; reduce heat and simmer approximately 10 minutes or until vegetable are tender. Add the spinach; simmer 1 to 2 minutes more or until spinach wilts.

Italian Roasted Vegetable Chicken Wraps

Loaded with Italian flavors, these colorful lunch options get an extra boost from fresh tomato-basil sauce! Pair these wraps with a serving of Phase One-approved fruit to complete your lunch.

Serves: 4

Ingredients

2 teaspoons Simply Organic Italian seasoning blend, divided

- 1 small red bell pepper, seeded and cut into strips
- 1 small green bell pepper, seeded and cut into strips
- 6 ounces Portobello mushrooms, washed and sliced
- 1 cup cooked shredded chicken breast
- 3 cups diced Roma tomatoes, flesh only
- 1 cup freshly basil leaves, coarsely chopped
- 8 slices sprouted-grain bread, lightly toasted

Preparation

Preheat oven to 425. On a 15x10x1 inch baking sheet, arrange peppers, mushrooms and cooked chicken, being careful not to crowd the pan. Sprinkle on 1 teaspoon Italian seasoning blend. Roast for 15 minutes, stirring 2 or 3 times, until tender and lightly browned.

In the meantime, place 1 cup diced tomatoes, the basil and remaining teaspoon Italian seasoning blend in a food processor. Process until smooth. Combine with remaining 2 cups diced tomatoes to create sauce.

Divide roasted vegetable and chicken between 4 slices of toasted bread, top with remaining slices. Serve sandwiches with individual bowls of sauce, heated if desired, for dipping.

Chicken-Mango Salad Wraps

Bursting with tropical flavors, these bright wraps combine your Phase One grain, fruit, vegetable and protein servings into one on-the-go lunch option!

Serves: 4

Ingredients

- 1 pound chicken strips, boneless, skinless
- 2 tablespoons Simply Organic Gumbo Base seasoning
- 4 cups mixed salad greens OR baby spinach leaves
- 1 cup chopped mango
- ¾ cup sliced red onion, separated into rings
- ½ cup green bell pepper
- 1 cup fresh raspberries, washed
- 2 tablespoons balsamic vinegar
- 4 spelt or sprouted-grain tortillas

Preparation

Preheat your broiler; line the broiler pan with foil. In a plastic freezer bag, toss chicken strips with Gumbo Base seasoning blend. Place onto prepared broiler pan and cook, approximately 4 inches from heat, until cooked through and no pink remains (170 degrees). Remove and set aside.

Meanwhile, place raspberries and balsamic vinegar in a food processor and process until smooth.

Divide salad greens evenly between each tortilla. Top with chicken, drizzle with raspberry-vinegar sauce and roll up. Serve immediately or pack with an ice pack in lunch containers.

Quinoa-Bean Salad

A delicious meat-free option, this satisfying salad is great for warmer days when you don't want to heat up the kitchen. Cook in the morning when temperatures are cooler – the salad will be perfectly chilled by lunchtime! Serve with the fruit of your choice to round out this Phase One lunch.

Serves: 4

Ingredients

- 1 cup chicken broth, homemade or canned (no artificial ingredients)
- ½ cup quinoa, rinsed
- 1 cup chopped bell pepper (any color)
- 2 medium fresh tomatoes, seeded and chopped
- 1 can (15 ounces) garbanzo beans (chickpeas), rinsed and drained
- ½ cup fresh green onions, chopped
- 2 tablespoons chopped fresh mint leaves
- 2 tablespoons chopped fresh parsley
- 2 tablespoons freshly squeezed lemon juice
- ¼ teaspoon EACH sea salt and freshly cracked black pepper

Preparation

In a saucepan, combine broth and quinoa; bring to a boil and reduce heat. Simmer covered for approximately 10 minutes or until broth has been absorbed and quinoa is tender. Fluff with a fork; set aside.

In the meantime, combine peppers, tomatoes, beans, onions, mint and parsley in a serving bowl. Add the cooked quinoa, lemon juice, salt and pepper. Toss to coat, taste for seasoning and adjust if desired. Chill for at least 2 hours before serving.

Peach Chicken Salad with Strawberry Dressing

Light and flavorful, this quick lunch is sped up by pre-cooking the chicken. See notes for poaching instructions. Serve with a sprouted-grain roll or bagel to round out your Phase One lunch.

Serves: 4

Ingredients

- 3 cups sliced strawberries, hulled, divided
- 2 tablespoons balsamic vinegar
- 6 cups baby spinach, arugula or mixed salad greens, rinsed and patted dry
- 1 pound cooked boneless skinless chicken breasts (see Note)
- 1 fresh peach, peeled and sliced
- 2 tablespoons chopped fresh green onions

Preparation

In a food processor, combine 2 cups strawberries and the balsamic vinegar. Process until smooth; set aside.

Divide the salad greens between four plates. Top with chicken, peach slices, remaining strawberries and green onions. Drizzle with strawberry-vinegar puree; serve immediately with rolls.

Note:

To poach chicken breasts, cover with water in a large saucepan and simmer, uncovered, until cooked through and no pink remains (a meat thermometer should register 170 degrees). Slice into strips and refrigerate immediately if preparing ahead of time. To use, reheat in the microwave or oven until temperature again reaches 170 to ensure safety.

Chickpea Vegetable Bagel Sandwiches

Great for vegetarians or anytime you need a meatless meal, these surprisingly hearty yet light sandwiches offer the great flavor of garlic hummus without the fat of added oils! Serve with an approved fruit choice to round out this Phase One lunch.

Serves: 4

Ingredients

- 1 cup canned chickpeas (garbanzo beans), drained and rinsed
- 1 teaspoon fresh minced garlic
- 4 sprouted-grain bagels, split and toasted
- 2 cups baby spinach leaves or mixed salad greens, washed and patted dry
- 2 fresh Roma tomatoes, sliced
- ¾ cup sliced fresh cucumber
- ¼ cup thinly sliced red onion
- ½ cup fresh green bell pepper, cut into strips

Preparation

In a food processor, process chickpeas and garlic until smooth and spreadable. Spread approximately 1 tablespoon onto each side of each split bagel. Later bottom bagel slices with ½ cup greens, tomatoes, cucumbers, onions and peppers. Top with remaining slices, press lightly and serve immediately alongside fruit of choice.

Phase One Dinners

Smoky Spicy BLT Pasta Salad

A delicious and zesty twist on the diner-classic sandwich, this Phase One-friendly dinner is ideal for warm-weather evenings when you don't want to heat up the kitchen too much! To make this salad kid-friendly, use very mild salsa and leave out the jalapenos.

Serves: 4 to 6

Ingredients

- 1 box (16 ounces) brown-rice or spelt pasta, any shape
- 1 package (1 pound) turkey bacon, cooked and crumbled (nitrate-free)
- 1 pound Roma tomatoes, seeded and chopped
- 1 cup chopped green onions
- 2 tablespoons chopped fresh jalapeno peppers (see Note)
- 4 cups lettuce, washed, dried and torn (see Note)
- 1 jar (14 ounces) red or green salsa (no artificial ingredients or sugar)

Preparation

In a large pot of lightly salted boiling water, follow package directions and cook pasta until al dente (firm but cooked through). Using a colander, immediately rinse with cold water and place in refrigerator until needed.

In the meantime, in a large serving bowl, combine crumbled turkey bacon, tomatoes, green onions, jalapenos and salsa. Add the pasta and stir to thoroughly incorporate.

At this stage, the salad can be refrigerated for a few hours or overnight; this saves time as well as allowing the pasta to soak up plenty of flavor from the salsa.

At serving time, add the lettuce, toss and serve immediately.

Note:

When handling jalapeno peppers, use caution; their oils can badly sting the eyes.

Any type of lettuce except for Iceberg is acceptable for this recipe. Some great choices include baby spinach, Romaine and arugula.

Individual Tortilla Pizzas

Dieting doesn't mean boring! Even kids will get excited about eating healthy when they get their own mini pizzas!

Serves: 4

Ingredients

- 4 large brown rice or spelt tortillas
- 2 cups chopped Roma tomatoes
- ½ cup chopped fresh basil leaves
- 1 teaspoon Simply Organic Italian seasoning blend

Toppings:

- Turkey bacon (nitrate-free), cooked and crumbled
- Deli meats (nitrate-free), sliced into strips
- Cooked and crumbled ground beef, turkey or chicken
- Green or white onions, thinly sliced
- Fresh bell peppers, sliced into strips
- Fresh button mushrooms, sliced
- Fresh jalapenos, seeded and sliced or chopped
- Baby spinach leaves, washed and dried
- Fresh Roma tomatoes, sliced
- Fresh basil leaves, whole or coarsely torn
- Red pepper flakes

Preparation

In a large nonstick skillet, briefly toast the tortillas to firm and crisp slightly. Set aside.

Preheat oven to 400 degrees.

In a food processor, process 2 cups chopped Roma tomatoes, ½ cup basil leaves and Italian seasoning to form a paste. Spread approximately 2 tablespoons over each prepared tortilla.

Assemble individual pizzas using the toppings of your choice – be sure to include at least 1 protein and 1 vegetable to ensure Phase One-compatibility.

Place assembled pizzas on a large baking sheet and bake for 4 to 7 minutes, or until toppings are lightly browned but not burned. Serve immediately.

Steamed Halibut with Quinoa and Tomatoes

This delicious and simple take on fish lightly sautés cherry tomatoes to retain all their fresh flavor.

Serves: 4

Ingredients

- 1 cup quinoa, rinsed and soaked if necessary
- 4 halibut fillets, skinless, approximately 6 ounces each
- 2 pints fresh cherry tomatoes, washed
- 2 tablespoons (or more as needed) chicken stock, homemade or packaged
- ¼ cup chopped fresh dill
- 2 tablespoons chopped fresh parsley
- Sea salt and freshly cracked black pepper

Preparation

Cook quinoa as directed on package; fluff with a fork and set aside.

In a large pot of water, poach halibut fillets by submerging them in water, bringing the water to a boil, reducing the heat and simmering, uncovered, until fish is opaque, cooked through and flakes easily with a fork (145 degrees). Remove, drain and set aside.

In a large, nonstick skillet, heat chicken stock. Add cherry tomatoes and sauté, stirring very frequently, until softened, approximately 6 minutes. Add dill and parsley during last minute of cooking to avoid burning herbs.

To serve, plate each halibut fillet and season to taste with salt and pepper. Add a serving of quinoa and spoon sautéed tomatoes over each fillet.

Basil-Lemongrass Chicken Stir-Fry

Bursting with fresh flavor but without the cornstarch and sugar common to many stir-fry recipes, this delicious Asian-inspired dish is a wonderfully fast Phase One option!

Serves: 4

Ingredients

- 1 cup brown rice, uncooked
- ½ cup (or more as needed) chicken stock, homemade or packaged); divided
- 1 ½ cups fresh green beans
- 1 ½ cups fresh yellow (wax) beans
- 1 ½ cups baby carrots OR sliced carrots
- 2 tablespoons green or white onion, finely minced
- 1 pound chicken breasts, boneless, skinless, cut into bite-size strips
- Freshly cracked black pepper to taste
- 1 teaspoon minced fresh garlic
- ¼ cup fresh lemongrass, minced
- 2 tablespoons grated lime zest
- ¼ cup fresh basil leaves, chopped or sliced into ribbons
- Additional lime zest and basil, for garnish, if desired

Preparation

Prepare brown rice according to directions on package.

As the rice cooks, heat ¼ cup chicken stock in a large, nonstick wok or skillet over medium heat. Add the onion and stir-fry for 1 to 2 minutes or until fragrant but not burned.

Add the chicken, black pepper as desired and lemongrass; cook and stir for approximately 6 to 10 minutes or until chicken is cooked through and no pink remains (160 degrees). During the last minute of cooking, add garlic, lime zest and basil.

In another large nonstick wok or skillet, heat remaining ¼ cup chicken stock and stir-fry beans and carrots until crisp-tender.

To serve, divide the rice between 4 plates or bowls; top with portions of chicken and vegetables. Sprinkle on additional basil and lime zest, if desired.

Chicken with Wild Rice and Broccoli

Simple and appealing even to picky eaters, this Phase One dinner can be put together in a flash by using leftovers! A quick stir-fry revives leftover wild rice and chicken and infuses them with delicious Italian flavors.

Serves: 4

Ingredients

- 3 cups cooked wild rice
- 3 cups cooked white-meat chicken, cubed or shredded (see Note)
- ½ cup chicken stock, homemade or packaged, no artificial ingredients
- 1 tablespoon Simply Organic Italian seasoning blend
- 1 tablespoon fresh basil, chopped
- 1 tablespoon fresh oregano, chopped
- 1 pound broccoli florets, fresh or frozen
- 1 ½ cups fresh Roma tomatoes, seeded and chopped

Preparation

In a very large, deep, nonstick skillet, heat chicken stock and stir-fry wild rice, chicken and Italian seasoning until heated through (see note). Add fresh basil and oregano during the last minute of cooking.

In the meantime, place broccoli in a steamer basket over a pot of boiling water OR in a partially covered, microwave-safe dish with approximately 1 cup of water. Steam until bright and crisp-tender.

Add the tomatoes to chicken-wild rice mixture in skillet; stir to combine. Divide between 4 plates alongside steamed broccoli; serve immediately.

Broiled Halibut with Salsa Verde

Ideal anytime you're craving bold flavor but want something a bit different, this light, flavorful dish is made quick through the use of purchased salsa, but bursting with the bright flavors of fresh cilantro, lime and chiles!

Serves: 6

Ingredients

- 6 halibut fillets, approximately 1 inch thick
- 2 tablespoons Simply Organic Southwest Taco seasoning blend
- 1 large (14 to 16 ounce) jar green salsa (all-natural, no sugar added)
- 1 fresh jalapeno pepper, seeded and chopped
- ¼ cup fresh cilantro, coarsely chopped
- 2 cloves fresh garlic, minced
- 2 tablespoons freshly grated lime zest
- 2 large Roma tomatoes, seeded and chopped
- Additional lime zest and cilantro, if desired, for garnish

Preparation

Preheat broiler.

Rub the halibut fillets with seasoning blend; place on a nonstick baking pan and broil approximately 8 to 10 minutes, carefully flipping halfway through cooking, until fish is opaque and flakes easily with a fork (145 degrees).

In the meantime, place jalapeno, cilantro, garlic and lime zest in a food processor; process until a paste is formed. Place the salsa in a small bowl; stir in jalapeno-lime paste to combine flavors.

Plate each broiled fillet; spoon salsa mixture over top and sprinkle with chopped tomatoes. Garnish with additional lime zest and cilantro, if desired.

Asian-Inspired Beef Stir Fry

As fast as any takeout restaurant, better for you and better tasting, this quick stir fry is a win-win-win!

Serves: 4

Ingredients

- 1 cup uncooked brown rice
- ¼ cup (or more if needed) chicken stock, homemade or packaged
- 2 tablespoons finely chopped onion
- 1 tablespoon fresh minced garlic
- 1 pound lean top round beef steak, sliced against the grain into thin strips
- 2 teaspoons Simply Organic Orange Ginger seasoning blend
- 2 cups fresh snow pea pods, trimmed
- 1 cup fresh sliced mushrooms
- ¼ cup sliced fresh lemongrass, optional, for garnish

Preparation

Cook the rice as directed on package.

In the meantime, heat chicken stock in a large, nonstick wok or skillet.

Add the onion and garlic; stir-fry for 1 minute or until fragrant but not browned. Add the beef strips and seasoning blend and cook, stirring constantly, until beef is halfway cooked, approximately 3 to 4 minutes.

Add the snow peas and mushrooms; continue cooking and stirring, adding chicken broth if necessary, until beef is cooked to desired doneness (at least 145 degrees) and vegetables are crisp-tender.

To serve, divide the rice between 4 bowls or plates; spoon beef-vegetable mixture over top and garnish with lemongrass if desired.

Grilled Quesadillas with Chicken and Black Beans

A real kid-pleaser and great for entertaining outdoors, these grilled quesadillas are packed with so much flavor, you'll never miss the fat!

Serves: 4

Ingredients

- 8 large brown-rice or spelt tortillas
- 1 can (15 ounces) no-salt-added black beans, rinsed and drained, *divided*
- 3 cups cooked, shredded chicken (see Note)
- 1 jar (14 ounces) prepared salsa (no sugar or salt added)
- 1 tablespoon plus 1 teaspoon Simply Organic Southwest Taco seasoning blend, *divided*
- 1 cup chopped fresh Roma tomatoes
- ¼ cup fresh cilantro leaves, chopped
- 1 tablespoon freshly grated lime zest

Preparation

Preheat your grill to medium heat or prepare medium-hot coals.

In a food processor, process half of the black beans and 1 teaspoon of seasoning blend until a paste forms.

In a small saucepan, combine shredded chicken, remaining seasoning blend and prepared salsa. Bring to a boil, reduce heat and simmer for 5 minutes to combine flavors.

Spread each tortilla with seasoned bean paste. In a bowl, combine shredded chicken-salsa mixture, tomatoes, cilantro and lime zest. Spoon the mixture over 4 prepared tortillas, then place remaining tortillas on top. Press lightly to seal.

Place quesadillas onto prepared grill or grill pan and cook for 1 minute on each side or until barely golden and crisped. Carefully remove and serve immediately.

Note:

If you're afraid of quesadillas sticking on a bare grill, you may want to use a nonstick grill grate (available at kitchen supply stores). This recipe can also be made indoors using a nonstick grill pan or counter-top grill.

If you don't have leftover chicken on hand, poach 3 to 4 boneless, skinless chicken breasts in water until cooked through and no pink remains (160 degrees); let cool slightly, shred and proceed as directed.

Italian Chicken Sandwiches

Instead of the unwanted fat of most sandwich spreads, this quick, brightly flavored Phase One dinner relies on pureed, garlic-flavored garbanzo beans to add protein and tons of Mediterranean flavor!

Serves: 4

Ingredients

- 4 boneless, skinless chicken breasts
- 1 tablespoon Simply Organic Italian seasoning blend
- ¼ cup chicken stock, homemade or packaged, no artificial ingredients
- 1 ½ cups canned garbanzo beans (chickpeas), rinsed and drained
- 1 tablespoon fresh garlic, minced
- 2 large Roma tomatoes, thickly sliced
- ¼ cup fresh basil, chopped
- ¼ cup fresh oregano, chopped
- 8 thick slices sprouted-grain bread, toasted

Preparation

In a large, nonstick skillet, heat chicken stock. Sprinkle seasoning blend over chicken breasts, add to skillet and cook approximately 4 minutes per side, or until cooked through and no pink remains (160 degrees).

In the meantime, place garbanzo beans and garlic in a food processor and process into a paste. Spread one side of each slice of toasted bread with bean mixture.

To assemble, place a chicken breast on 4 slices of prepared bread; top with tomato slices, fresh basil and oregano; serve immediately.

Vegetable-Turkey Wild Rice Soup

Filled with comforting flavor and ideal for chilly evenings, this soup features low-fat ground turkey and plenty of vegetables for a quick and well-rounded Phase One dinner!

Serves: 4

Ingredients

- 1 pound ground white-meat turkey
- 2 yellow onions, chopped
- 2 cups chopped celery (leaves included)
- 2 cups chopped fresh carrots
- 2 cloves fresh minced garlic
- 1 tablespoon chopped fresh thyme
- 1 tablespoon chopped fresh rosemary
- 3 cups organic wild rice, cooked
- 6 cups chicken stock, homemade or packaged (no artificial ingredients)

Preparation

In a large nonstick stockpot over medium heat, cook the ground turkey and onions until turkey is fully cooked through and no pink remains and onions are translucent and fragrant. Add celery, carrots, garlic, thyme, rosemary, wild rice and chicken stock; bring to a boil.

Reduce heat and simmer, uncovered, approximately 15 minutes or until vegetables are tender. Serve immediately.

Phase One Snacks

Zesty Orange-Strawberry Snack

Ingredients

- 1 cup fresh strawberries, hulled and sliced
- 1 medium orange, peeled and sectioned
- 1 tablespoon fresh lemon juice

Preparation

Combine all ingredients in a small bowl or resealable lunch container; toss to coat. Chill until serving.

Spiced Pears

Ingredients

- 1 firm, ripe Bosc pear, sliced
- ⅛ teaspoon cinnamon
- Pinch of nutmeg

Preparation

Sprinkle spices onto pear slices; place in a zippered plastic bag or resealable lunch container Chill until serving.

Zesty Citrus Melon

Ingredients

- 1 cup cubed melon (watermelon, honeydew or cantaloupe)
- ¼ teaspoon chili powder (or more to taste)
- 1 tablespoon fresh lime juice

Preparation

Sprinkle the melon cubes with chili powder and drizzle with lime juice; toss to coat and store in a zippered plastic bag or resealable lunch container. Chill until serving.

Chapter 2

Phase 2

High Protein & Veggies, Low Carb, Low Fat Meals

Phase Two Breakfasts

Cucumber-Kale Frittata

Loaded with healthy protein and vegetables, this frittata is a great way to make your everyday omelet a little more special!

Serves: 4

Ingredients

- 2 ¼ cups egg white or packaged, refrigerated egg white
- 2 tablespoons chopped fresh oregano
- 2 tablespoons chopped fresh basil
- ½ teaspoon sea salt
- ¼ teaspoon freshly cracked black pepper
- 1 tablespoon homemade or packaged chicken stock (no artificial ingredients)
- 2 cups frozen chopped spinach, thawed and drained
- ¾ cup chopped fresh cucumbers

Preparation

Preheat oven to 375. In a large bowl, whisk together eggs, oregano, basil, salt and pepper.

In a large nonstick, oven-safe skillet, cook the spinach and cucumbers in chicken broth until heated through, approximately 3 minutes. Drain off any excess liquid.

Pour egg mixture into skillet; tilt to evenly distribute eggs. Place skillet in preheated oven and cook for approximately 20 minutes, or until top is browned and eggs are set and cooked through (160 degrees).

Cut into wedges and serve hot.

Smoky Turkey-Bacon Scrambled Eggs

A quick and easy dish for one, this delicious yet simple scramble combines your protein and vegetable servings for a complete Phase Two breakfast!

Serves: 1

Ingredients

- 4 egg whites (or refrigerated, pasteurized liquid egg whites)
- 3 slices turkey bacon (nitrate-free), cooked and crumbled
- 1 teaspoon water
- ½ teaspoon chili powder
- ¼ teaspoon cumin
- 1 cup sliced fresh bell pepper, any color
- Sea salt and freshly cracked black pepper to taste
- 1 ½ cups fresh baby spinach leaves, washed and patted dry

Preparation

In a bowl, whisk together eggs, water, chili powder, cumin, salt and pepper.

In a nonstick skillet over medium heat, cook and stir eggs until partially set. Add the bacon and peppers; continue cooking until eggs are set and cooked through (160 degrees). Serve atop baby spinach.

Grab-and-Go Deli Roll-Ups

Ideal for busy mornings since they can be fully prepared the night before, these quick breakfast snacks should be made with nitrate-free deli meat only.

Serves: 1

Ingredients

- 6 slices deli meat (roast beef, turkey or chicken)
- Assorted fresh sliced vegetables (carrots, celery, spinach, bell peppers, jalapeno peppers, mushrooms, sweet onions) (see Note)

Preparation

Place a small amount of your vegetables of choice in the middle of each slice of deli meat and roll up. Keep thoroughly chilled until serving.

Note:

If using fresh jalapeno peppers, use caution. Remove seeds and membranes, and be careful not to touch your eyes until you've washed your hands, as the oils in jalapenos can burn severely.

Burgers for Breakfast

Delicious and loaded with protein, these lean burgers are a fun change of pace when served with a southwest-spiced vegetable sauté.

Serves: 4

Ingredients

- 1 pound baby spinach leaves, washed and dried
- 4 (¼ pound) patties lean ground beef (see Note)
- 2 cups fresh bell peppers, sliced into strips (any color)
- 2 teaspoons chicken broth, homemade or packaged (no artificial ingredients)
- 1 teaspoon Simply Organic Southwest Taco seasoning blend
- Sea salt and freshly cracked black pepper, to taste, if desired

Preparation

In a large nonstick skillet, cook the burger patties until desired doneness is reached (at least 160 degrees). Set aside.

In another large nonstick skillet, stir-fry the peppers, seasoning blend and salt and pepper if desired until peppers are just beginning to become tender, approximately 2 minutes. Add the spinach leaves; cover and remove from the heat. Allow skillet to stand until spinach has wilted, approximately 4 minutes. Serve each burger patty atop spinach-pepper mixture.

Note:

To save time in the morning, purchase pre-formed burger patties in the freezer section. Be sure to purchase only those with no fillers or additives, and choose organic, grass-fed options when available.

Southwest Chicken-Lettuce "Wraps"

A great eat-on-the-go option, these zesty wraps include all you need for a flavorful and Phase Two-friendly breakfast!

Serves: 4

Ingredients

- 4 boneless, skinless chicken breasts
- 1 tablespoon chili powder
- 1 teaspoon cumin
- Crushed red pepper flakes to taste
- 1 fresh lime, cut into 4 wedges
- 4 (or more as needed) large leaves lettuce (see Note)

Preparation

In a large pan, poach chicken breasts in water until cooked through and no pink remains (160 degrees).

Assemble wraps by placing 1 chicken breast on each lettuce leaf, using more leaves if necessary. Sprinkle seasonings over chicken; juice a lime wedge over each and roll up to serve.

Note:

Any variety of lettuce is acceptable except for Iceberg. Some great wrapping choices include Bibb and Boston.

Italian Egg Scramble with Chicken

In addition to being a complete Phase Two breakfast option, this delicious scramble is a great way to use up leftover chicken!

Serves: 4

Ingredients

- 8 egg whites (or refrigerated, pasteurized liquid egg whites)
- 1 teaspoon water
- 1 pound boneless, skinless chicken breasts
- 1 tablespoon Simply Organic Italian seasoning blend
- 2 tablespoons fresh basil, chopped
- ¼ teaspoon red pepper flakes
- Sea salt and black pepper to taste (optional)

Preparation

Preheat your broiler and line broiler pan with aluminum foil. Rub chicken breasts with the Italian seasoning blend and broil approximately 4 inches from heat source until cooked through and no pink remains (170 degrees). Remove, let cool slightly and chop.

In a bowl, whisk egg whites, water, fresh basil and red pepper flakes. Pour mixture into a large nonstick skillet over medium heat and cook, stirring frequently, until partially set. Add chicken, stir to combine, and continue cooking until eggs are cooked through (160 degrees) and set. Serve immediately.

Greek Scrambled Eggs

Exotic and fun for breakfast, this dish highlights all the great flavors of Greece without any dairy or added fat!

Serves: 4

Ingredients

- 12 egg whites (or pasteurized, refrigerated liquid egg whites)
- 2 tablespoons fresh parsley, minced
- 3 tablespoons fresh mint leaves, minced
- 2 teaspoons fresh dill, minced
- 3 tablespoons green onions, minced
- 2 cups fresh baby spinach leaves, washed and dried, packed
- 1 tablespoon chicken broth (homemade or packaged, no artificial ingredients)
- 2 cup chopped cucumber
- Sea salt and freshly cracked black pepper to taste

Preparation

In a large bowl, combine eggs, parsley, mint and green onions with a wire whisk. In a large nonstick skillet over medium heat, heat the chicken broth and stir-fry spinach leaves for approximately 2 to 3 minutes or until wilted. Add the eggs and continue to cook, stirring, until eggs are nearly set. Add tomatoes and cucumbers, stir to combine, and continue cooking until eggs are set and cooked through (160 degrees).

Serve immediately, seasoned as desired with sea salt and pepper.

Poached Flounder and Eggs with Vegetables

While fish isn't a common choice for breakfast, it's an everyday treat in many parts of the world! By poaching both the fish and eggs, you avoid the extra fat that usually accompanies a fish-based meal, and mushrooms and onions add a burst of extra-hearty flavor. This Phase Two breakfast is ideal for cold mornings when you have a bit of time to make something special!

Serves: 4

Ingredients

- 1 pound flounder fillets (see Note)
- 8 egg whites (or pasteurized, refrigerated liquid egg whites)
- 1 teaspoon water
- Vegetable broth or stock, homemade or packaged (no artificial ingredients)
- 1 cup sliced fresh mushrooms
- 1 cup coarsely chopped red onions
- 2 tablespoons broth or stock
- Sea salt and freshly cracked black pepper to taste

Preparation

In a large stockpot, heat as much broth as needed to fully cover fish fillets. When the broth is simmering, gently add fillets. Poach for approximately 5 minutes, or until done; fish should be opaque and flake easily.

In the meantime, heat 2 tablespoons broth in a nonstick skillet over medium heat. Add the mushrooms and onions and stir-fry until tender and lightly browned. Set aside.

Scramble eggs by whisking whites and water in a large bowl. In the same nonstick skillet used to stir-fry vegetables, cook and stir eggs until set and cooked through (160 degrees).

Assemble plates by placing one poached fillet and one serving of eggs; spoon mushroom-onion mixture over the top and season to taste with salt and pepper. Serve immediately.

Steak Frittata

Combining the classic flavors of a steak-and-egg breakfast into an even heartier dish, this frittata is traditionally made in an oiled cast-iron skillet. To achieve the same results without additional fats, use a good-quality nonstick and oven-safe skillet.

Serves: 4 to 6

Ingredients

- 2 small steak filets (approximately 3 ounces each), cooked (see Note)
- 12 egg whites (or pasteurized, refrigerated egg whites)
- 2 teaspoons water
- 2 teaspoons Simply Organic Spicy Steak seasoning blend
- ½ cup red onion, chopped or sliced
- ¾ cup fresh bell pepper, sliced into strips (any color)
- ½ cup sliced fresh mushrooms
- 1 teaspoon fresh minced garlic
- 2 tablespoons chicken stock (homemade or packaged, no artificial ingredients)
- Sea salt and freshly cracked black pepper

Preparation

Preheat over to 400 degrees.

In a large bowl, whisk egg whites with water and Spicy Steak seasoning blend.

Cut cooked steaks into bite-sized pieces; set aside.

In a large, nonstick, oven-safe skillet, stir-fry onion, peppers and mushrooms until barely tender, approximately 5 minutes. Add garlic and cook another 1 to 2 minutes, until garlic is fragrant but not burned. Add the steak and stir to combine.

Pour egg mixture over mixture in skillet; stir to combine. Place skillet in preheated over and cook for 10 to 15 minutes, checking after 10 minutes, until eggs are cooked through and set (160 degrees). Cut frittata into wedges to serve; season to taste with salt and pepper.

Note:

This recipe is great for using up leftover steaks. If you need to cook the steaks, do it quickly and without added fat by broiling them, approximately 4 inches from the heat and turning once during cooking, until their internal temperature reaches 150 degrees and the steaks are done to your liking.

Steak and Eggs

A longtime diner favorite, this classic breakfast gets a healthy upgrade through broiling and poaching instead of traditional fat-laden cooking methods! By pairing it with a simple salad, this 'dinner for breakfast' luxury becomes a complete Phase Two meal option.

Serves: 4

Ingredients

- 4 lean steaks (cut of your choice)
- 8 egg whites (or refrigerated, pasteurized egg whites)
- 2 tablespoons Simply Organic Spicy OR regular Steak Seasoning
- 4 cups baby spinach leaves, washed and patted dry
- 1 cup sliced mushrooms
- ½ cup sliced red onions, separated into rings
- 1 to 2 tablespoons chicken stock, homemade or packaged (no artificial ingredients)
- Sea salt and freshly cracked black pepper (as desired)

Preparation

Preheat your broiler and line a broiler pan with aluminum foil (not necessary if using a nonstick broiler pan).

Rub each steak with Simply Organic seasoning. Broil, approximately 5 to 6 inches from heat source (see Note) and turning once during cooking, until meat reaches desired doneness (at least 145 degrees). Remove and allow to rest 3 minutes before serving.

(Continued on next page)

Preparation (continued)

In the meantime, bring a large pot of lightly salted water to a simmer. Working in small batches, slide 1 egg white at a time into the water. Cook until opaque and set; remove with a slotted spoon. Continue until all egg whites have been poached. (See Note)

In a nonstick skillet over medium heat, stir-fry the mushrooms and onions in chicken broth, adding additional broth by teaspoons if vegetables begin to burn.

To serve, plate each steak with two egg whites. Plate spinach leaves; top with sautéed mushroom-onion mixture. Season to taste and serve immediately.

Note:

Broiling times will depend on the cut and thickness of the steak you choose, as well as individual broilers. If you notice your steaks are browning before the interior is cooked to your liking, move steaks further from the heat source.

Poaching eggs can be difficult, especially for beginners. An egg-poaching ring, a simple metal ring that attaches to the side of a cooking pot and creates perfectly round eggs, is a great tool for this recipe. Egg-poaching rings are available online and at kitchen-supply stores.

Phase Two Lunches

Quick-Cook Chicken with Broccoli Soup

The secret to keeping this meal lunch-friendly is purchasing thin chicken cutlets. If you don't see any in the meat case, ask your butcher for recommendations or if a custom cut is possible.

Serves: 4

Ingredients

- 1 pound chicken cutlets, pounded if necessary (see Note)
- 4 tablespoons chicken stock (homemade or packaged), *divided*
- 1 tablespoon Simply Organic Citrus 'n' Herb seasoning blend
- 1 red onion, finely chopped
- 2 heads fresh broccoli, coarsely chopped (stems included)
- 2 quarts water OR chicken stock (see Note)
- Sea salt and freshly cracked black pepper, to taste

Preparation

Place water or broth in a large stockpot; bring to a boil.

While water boils, rub chicken cutlets with seasoning blend. Heat 2 tablespoons of stock in a nonstick skillet and sauté chicken until done and no pink remains (160 degrees). Set aside.

In a large nonstick skillet, add the remaining 2 tablespoons stock and cook the onion until soft and translucent, between 10 and 15 minutes. Add the broccoli and stir-fry approximately 4 minutes or until crisp-tender.

Add the vegetable mixture to the stockpot; simmer until broccoli is soft. Drain. Working in small batches, puree in a food processor until smooth and creamy. Serve immediately, alongside seasoned chicken cutlets.

Note:

For more uniform cooking, pound chicken to an even thickness by placing cutlets in a durable zipper-close plastic freezer bag and pounding with a heavy cast-iron skillet or meat mallet. Discard the bag.

Water is fine for this recipe, but using chicken stock will give your soup a richer flavor.

Southwest Turkey Burger Wraps

Spicy and satisfying, these wraps can be made kid-friendly by leaving out the jalapenos. They're rather delicate because no grains are used as fillers – wrapping up the crumbled turkey burger is much easier than trying to form patties.

Serves: 6

Ingredients

- 1 ½ pounds ground turkey
- 1 white onion, finely chopped
- 2 tablespoons finely chopped fresh jalapeno peppers
- 1 tablespoon chili powder
- 1 teaspoon cumin
- ¼ cup fresh cilantro, coarsely chopped
- 1 fresh lime, cut into wedges
- 6 (or more as needed) large lettuce leaves (any variety except Iceberg) (see Note)

Preparation

In a large nonstick skillet, crumble and cook the turkey burger, jalapenos, onion, chili powder and cumin until cooked through and no pink remains (165 degrees). Stir in the cilantro.

To assemble, spoon a portion of the turkey mixture onto each lettuce leaf and roll up. Serve immediately with a lime wedge for juicing over the wraps.

Note:

While any type of lettuce can be used in this recipe, Bibb and Boston varieties typically have leaves, which are large enough to be used as wraps.

Grilled Chicken Salad with Garlic and Basil

To make this Phase Two lunch faster, pre-cook your chicken the night before and re-heat to 160 degrees before serving.

Serves: 4

Ingredients

- 12 ounces boneless, skinless chicken breasts, pounded (see Note)
- 2 tablespoons lemon juice, freshly squeezed
- 1 teaspoon dried oregano, crushed
- 1 teaspoon finely minced fresh garlic
- Sea salt and freshly cracked black pepper to taste
- 4 cups baby spinach leaves, washed and dried
- ½ cup fresh basil leaves
- 1 small red onion, sliced and separated into rings
- 2 cups bell pepper (any color), sliced into strips
- 2 celery stalks, chopped (leaves included)
- 3 tablespoons balsamic vinegar

Preparation

Heat a nonstick grill pan or a counter-top grill to medium heat. In a bowl, combine the lemon juice, oregano, garlic, salt and pepper. Add chicken and stir briefly to coat. Discard excess grilling sauce (see Note).

Grill the chicken over medium heat until cooked through and no pink remains (160 degrees), turning once during cooking. Cooking times will vary depending on thickness. Set aside.

In the meantime, combine the spinach leaves, basil, onion and peppers in a large bowl. Divide among four plates; top each salad serving with a chicken breast. Drizzle each serving with balsamic vinegar; serve immediately.

Note:

Pounding your chicken will allow for more uniform cooking. To reduce the risk of cross-contamination while pounding chicken, place chicken breasts in a heavy-duty, zipper-close plastic freezer bag, seal, and pound with the bottom of a heavy skillet or a meat mallet.

If you choose to cook your chicken ahead of time, you may use the grilling sauce as a marinade. Place pounded chicken breasts and grilling sauce ingredients in a bowl, cover with plastic wrap and refrigerate between 2 to 6 hours. Discard excess marinade and cook as directed.

Safety Tip: To ensure safety, always measure temperature using an instant-read meat thermometer inserted into the thickest portion of the meat.

Rosemary-Mustard Chicken Salad

With a deliciously unexpected flavor twist and several serving options, this lightly-dressed Phase Two lunch is an ideal way to use up leftover chicken!

Serves: 4

Ingredients

- 3 cups cubed or shredded cooked chicken breast, boneless, skinless (see Note)
- ⅓ cup chopped yellow onion
- 2 teaspoons chopped fresh rosemary
- 1 cup chopped fresh celery (leaves included)
- ¼ cup Dijon mustard
- Sea salt and freshly cracked black pepper to taste

Preparation

Serving options: 4 cups baby spinach leaves or mixed salad greens; 4 large leaves Bibb or Boston lettuce; individual resealable lunch containers

In a large bowl, combine the chicken, onion, rosemary, celery, salt and pepper. Add the mustard; toss to lightly coat all ingredients.

To serve, either plate atop salad greens, roll up in leaves of lettuce or pack into containers and refrigerate until serving.

Note:

If you don't have any leftover chicken on hand, you can quickly poach chicken breasts by simmering them in a deep skillet until cooked through and no pink remains (160 degrees). Shred or cube and proceed as directed.

Philly-Inspired Steak Wraps

With the beloved flavors of onions, peppers, mushrooms and steak but without the unwanted dairy or fat, these filling sandwiches are sure to be a hit with hearty eaters!

Serves: 4

Ingredients

- 1 pound top round steak (beef or buffalo)
- 1 tablespoon Simply Organic Steak seasoning blend
- 1 pound button mushrooms, rinsed and sliced
- 1 red onion, sliced thin and separated into rings
- 1 large green bell pepper, cut into strips
- 1 teaspoon finely minced garlic
- 2 tablespoons chicken stock (homemade or packaged; no artificial ingredients)
- 4 large leaves Bibb or Boston lettuce (see Note)

Preparation

Preheat your broiler.

If you don't have a nonstick broiler pan, line your broiler pan with aluminum foil.

Rub steak with seasoning blend and broil, approximately 4 inches from the heat, turning once, until desired doneness is reached (at least 145 degrees). Remove, let rest for at least 3 minutes, then slice into thin strips. Set aside.

In the meantime, in a large, nonstick skillet over medium heat, stir-fry the button mushrooms, onion and peppers in the chicken stock until barely crisp-tender, approximately 5 to 7 minutes. Add the garlic and cook an additional minute or until the garlic becomes fragrant but not burned.

Add the steak strips to pan with vegetables; toss lightly to combine. Divide the mixture between 4 large lettuce leaves; roll up and serve immediately.

Note:

If you prefer, you may serve the steak-and-vegetable mixture atop a bed of baby spinach leaves or mixed salad greens.

Bacon Salad with Arugula

This satisfying yet light Phase Two lunch option healthfully satisfies those bacon cravings!

Serves: 4

Ingredients

- 12 strips turkey bacon, nitrate-free, cooked and crumbled
- 4 cups arugula, washed and dried (see Note)
- 2 cups chopped cucumbers
- 1 tablespoon minced fresh chives
- ½ teaspoon minced fresh sage (or ¼ teaspoon dried)
- Sea salt and freshly cracked black pepper to taste (if desired)
- 2 tablespoons Dijon mustard
- 2 tablespoons balsamic vinegar

Preparation

In a large bowl, combine cooked turkey bacon, arugula, cucumbers, chives and sage; if desired, season to taste with salt and pepper.

In a small bowl, whisk together Dijon mustard and vinegar. Divide salad between 4 plates; drizzle with Dijon mixture and serve.

Note:

Arugula is prized for its peppery flavor, but using only arugula may be too strong for some diners. You can easily make this dish more mild by using a mix of arugula and baby spinach, mixed salad greens, Romaine, Bibb or Boston lettuce.

Cajun Fish Wraps

With its smoky, spicy Cajun flavors and lemon-dressed vegetables, this Phase Two lunch option is surprisingly simple yet completely satisfying! Pre-heating your baking sheet will give the fish fillets a delicious crunch.

Serves: 4

Ingredients

- 1 pound halibut or cod fillets, cut into 4 serving-size pieces
- 1 tablespoon Simply Organic Gumbo Base OR Jambalaya Seasoning blend
- 2 fresh lemons, each cut into 4 wedges
- 1 pound fresh or frozen broccoli florets
- Sea salt and freshly cracked black pepper to taste
- 4 (or more if needed) large leaves Bibb or Boston lettuce

Preparation

Preheat oven to 350 degrees. When oven is hot, place a nonstick sheet pan inside and heat it for 30 minutes.

Rub fish with seasoning blend of your choice. Working carefully, place each fish fillet on the heated baking sheet. Cook for 30 minutes or until fish is opaque and flakes easily with a fork (145 degrees).

(Continued on next page)

Preparation (continued)

In the meantime, steam the broccoli using a dedicated steamer, a steamer rack set over a pot of boiling water, or in the microwave (see Note for directions). When the vegetables are crisp-tender and brightly colored, remove from the heat and plate. Dress with the juice of 1 lemon wedge; add salt and pepper as desired.

When the fish is done and cool enough to handle safely, season each fillet with lemon juice, salt and pepper, roll up in a lettuce leaf and plate alongside steamed vegetables.

Note:

To steam vegetables in the microwave, place in a microwave-safe bowl or dish, add approximately ¾ cup water and partially cover, leaving an open area for steam to vent. Microwave on high until vegetables have brightened and are crisp-tender in texture.

If your fish comes out of the oven slightly soggy on the bottom, heat your broiler, turn fillets upside down and broil, watching carefully, until lightly browned.

Fish is notoriously for sticking to pans. Since no added oils are used in this recipe, be extremely gentle when removing fish from the baking sheet; a wide spatula works best.

Herbed Lamb Steaks with Cucumber Relish

While we typically think of lamb as a labor-intensive roast served on special occasions, there are plenty of smaller and leaner cuts available. This surprisingly quick Phase Two lunch option utilizes lean rump steaks for quick cooking and minimized fat content!

Serves: 4

Ingredients

- 4 boneless lamb rump steaks (3 ounces each)
- ⅔ cup chopped fresh parsley
- 3 tablespoons chopped fresh rosemary
- ¼ teaspoon onion salt
- 2 cups chopped fresh cucumbers (see Note)
- 1 tablespoon chopped fresh dill
- ½ lemon, for dressing

Preparation

Preheat your broiler (see Note). In a small bowl, combine parsley, rosemary and onion salt; rub generously on both sides of each steak working the mixture well into the meat.

Using a nonstick (or aluminum foil-lined) broiler pan, broil steaks approximately 5 inches from the heat until meat reaches desired doneness (at least 145 degrees). Allow the steaks to rest for 3 minutes before serving or cutting.

In the meantime, combine cucumbers and dill in a bowl; squeeze the lemon over the mixture and toss lightly to coat.

Plate each lamb steak and spoon relish over the top. Serve immediately, with extra lemon wedges for dressing if desired.

Note:

Cucumbers, due to their thin skins, are more likely to absorb toxic pesticides than other vegetables. If you purchase organic cucumbers, feel free to leave the skins on. If you purchase regular cucumbers, peeling is advised.

Working the herbs into the meat moistens them, which cuts down on the risk of burning before the lamb is cooked. If you notice that the herbs are browning too quickly, remove them from the broiler and finish cooking in a 350-degree oven.

Quick Garden Chicken Soup

Super-fast and a great way to use up leftovers, this soup delivers all the protein and vegetables required for a rounded Phase Two lunch. Place in thermos containers for a warm and satisfying meal on the go!

Serves: 4

Ingredients

- 2 cups cooked white-meat chicken, shredded or cubed (see Note)
- 4 cups chicken stock, homemade or packaged (no artificial ingredients)
- ½ cup chopped red onion
- 1 cup fresh sliced mushrooms
- 1 cup fresh red bell pepper, sliced into strips
- 1 clove garlic, finely minced or crushed
- 1 teaspoon Simply Organic Italian seasoning blend
- 2 cups fresh baby spinach leaves, washed and dried

Preparation

In a large saucepan, combine chicken, stock, onion, mushrooms, peppers, garlic and seasoning blend. Bring to a boil and simmer, uncovered, at least 7 minutes or until vegetable are crisp-tender.

Add spinach leaves, stir briefly, and continue cooking until spinach has wilted, approximately 2 minutes.

Serve immediately or pour into insulated thermos containers and keep hot until serving.

Note: This recipe is extremely versatile — virtually any leftover cooked meat and vegetables you have on hand can be used, in the same amounts, as long as they are Phase Two-friendly.

Fresh Herbed Tuna Salad

Refreshing and a nice change from traditional tuna salad, this Phase Two-friendly lunch option packs plenty of heart-healthy protein and vegetables!

Serves: 4

Ingredients

- 1 can (approximately 16 ounces) tuna in water, drained and flaked
- ¼ cup minced yellow onion
- 2 stalks fresh celery, chopped (greens included)
- ⅓ cup no-sugar-added pickle relish (optional)
- ¼ cup fresh chopped dill
- 2 tablespoons fresh chopped chives
- 2 tablespoons fresh chopped parsley
- 4 cups baby spinach leaves or mixed salad greens

Preparation

In a bowl, combine all ingredients except salad greens; mix well. Divide salad greens among four plates, spoon tuna salad on top and serve immediately. Refrigerate any leftovers.

Phase Two Dinners

Garlic Rosemary Beef Roast

Hearty and satisfying, this dish's garlic-tucking technique infuses the entire roast with great flavor!

Serves: 4 to 6

Ingredients

- 4 cloves garlic, cut into slivers
- 3 tablespoons chopped fresh rosemary
- Sea salt and freshly cracked black pepper to taste
- 1 tri-tip beef roast (approximately 3 pounds), trimmed of visible fat
- 1 ½ cups sliced button mushrooms
- 1 cup sweet bell pepper (any color), sliced into strips
- 1 cup sliced yellow onion
- 3 tablespoons chicken stock (homemade or packaged, no artificial ingredients)

Preparation

Preheat oven to 425. Place a wire rack in a roasting pan.

Using a small, sharp knife, poke shallow holes all over roast; insert a sliver of garlic into each hole. Rub roast with rosemary, salt and pepper. Place roast on rack and cook, checking after 30 minutes, for 30 to 60 minutes or until desired doneness is reached (at least 145 degrees). If your roast begins to brown before the inside is cooked, loosely tent the roast with aluminum foil.

Allow your roast to rest for 3 minutes before slicing.

In the meantime, in a large nonstick skillet, heat the chicken stock and stir-fry the vegetables until the mushrooms are lightly browned and the peppers and onions are browned and crisp- tender.

Slice your roast and serve along stir-fried vegetables; season with additional salt and pepper if desired. Spoon pan juices over servings and serve immediately.

Herbed Mustard Turkey Roast

Not just for holidays, this delicious and flavorful turkey roast is simple enough for any night of the week, yet special enough for entertaining! Using a bone-in breast infuses the meat with extra flavor.

Serves: 6

Ingredients

- 1 bone-in turkey breast, approximately 6 pounds, skin removed
- 3 cloves fresh garlic, minced
- 2 teaspoons dry mustard
- 1 tablespoon chopped fresh thyme
- 1 tablespoon chopped fresh rosemary
- 1 tablespoon chopped fresh sage
- Sea salt and freshly cracked black pepper to taste
- 1 bulb fennel, peeled and cut into ¼ inch thick slices
- 3 cups baby spinach leaves, washed and dried
- 3 to 4 tablespoons chicken stock, homemade or packaged (no artificial ingredients)

Preparation

Preheat your oven to 325 degrees. Combine the garlic, mustard, thyme, rosemary and sage; rub over turkey breast. Place on a wire rack in a roasting pan; roast for 1 hour, 45 minutes to 2 hours, or until cooked through and golden brown. An instant-read meat thermometer inserted in several of the thickest parts of the breast should read at least 165 degrees. If your roast begins to brown before it is cooked through, tent loosely with aluminum foil.

In the meantime, in a large nonstick skillet, heat the chicken stock and stir-fry fennel slices until tender, approximately 7 to 10 minutes. Add the spinach; cover and remove from heat to wilt spinach leaves.

Slice turkey; plate with stir-fried vegetable and serve immediately with pan drippings spooned over each plate.

Note:

If you can't find a bone-in breast without skin, your supermarket's butcher will remove it for you. You can also make this recipe with a boneless breast; reduce the cooking time and begin checking for doneness after 1 hour, 30 minutes.

When checking the internal temperature of bone-in cuts of meat, be careful not to touch the thermometer to the bone itself. Temperature readings should always be taken from the thickest portion of the meat itself.

Southwest Seasoned Steaks with Spinach-Jicama Salad

Smoky spices are paired with a bright and fresh salad for a great warm-weather Phase Two dinner option!

Serves: 4

Ingredients

- 4 lean beef or bison steaks
- 2 tablespoons Simply Organic Southwest Taco Seasoning blend
- ¾ cup chopped fresh cilantro, *divided*
- 4 cups baby spinach leaves, washed and dried
- 2 cups jicama, peeled and chopped or sliced into strips
- 1 fresh lime, halved
- Sea salt and freshly cracked black pepper to taste

Preparation

Preheat your broiler. Rub the steaks with seasoning blend. Using a nonstick broiler pan or one lined with aluminum foil, broil steaks approximately 4 inches from heat until desired doneness is reached (at least 145 degrees). Cooking times vary widely depending on the thickness of your steaks; watch carefully to avoid burning. Rest for 3 minutes before slicing or serving.

In the meantime, in a large bowl, toss together spinach, jicama and ¼ cup chopped cilantro. Squeeze lime over the salad and toss to coat. Divide between four plates; add a seasoned steak, top each steak with remaining cilantro and serve immediately.

Note:

Still rather unfamiliar but gaining popularity, jicama can be found in most large supermarkets' produce sections. Their flavor and texture is similar to an apple.

Asian-Spiced Grilled Chicken

Ideal for warm-weather evenings, this simple chicken dinner offers exotic flavor combinations and a well-rounded Phase Two option!

Serves: 4

Ingredients

- 4 boneless, skinless chicken breasts
- 3 tablespoons Simply Organic Orange Ginger seasoning blend, *divided*
- 2 pounds fresh broccoli, cut into bite-size pieces
- ¼ cup grated fresh ginger
- ½ cup chicken stock, homemade or purchased, no artificial ingredients
- ½ teaspoon crushed red pepper flakes (optional)

Preparation

Preheat a nonstick grill pan (or counter-top grill) over medium heat.

Rub the chicken with seasoning blend. Grill, turning once, until cooked through and no pink remains, approximately 4 to 7 minutes per side.

Cooking times will vary depending on the thickness of the meat; an instant-read meat thermometer inserted into the thickest portion of the breast should register at least 160 degrees. Remove from grill and set aside.

In the meantime, heat the chicken stock in a large, nonstick skillet over medium-high heat. Add the broccoli and ginger and cook, stirring constantly, until bright and crisp-tender.

Plate each chicken breast with a serving of gingered broccoli; sprinkle on red pepper flakes if desired and serve immediately.

Note:

While this recipe is just as delicious on an outdoor charcoal or gas grill, chicken breasts are notorious for sticking to grill racks unless they are well-oiled. In order to avoid added oils and fats, using an indoor, nonstick grill pan or counter-top grill is best.

Herbed Lemon Halibut with Green Beans

A fresh and flavorful dinner that's not too heavy, this Phase Two fish dish pairs beautifully with freshly steamed, simply-dressed green beans.

Serves: 6

Ingredients

- 6 halibut steaks, approximately 1 inch thick (see Note)
- 2 cloves minced garlic
- 1 tablespoon chopped fresh dill
- 1 tablespoon chopped fresh thyme
- 1 tablespoon chopped fresh basil
- ¼ teaspoon crushed red pepper flakes
- ¼ cup chopped yellow onion
- 3 to 5 fresh lemons, cut into ¾ inch thick slices
- 1 pound fresh green beans
- 1 cup chicken stock, homemade or packaged (no artificial ingredients)
- Additional lemon wedges, for serving

Preparation

Preheat your oven to 425 degrees. Line the bottom of a baking dish with lemon slices; place halibut steaks on top.

In a small bowl, combine garlic, dill, thyme, basil, red pepper flakes and chopped onion. Press the mixture on top of halibut steaks in baking dish; top herb mixture with additional lemon slices to cover each steak.

Bake for 14 to 20 minutes, depending on thickness, until fish is opaque and flakes easily with a fork (145 degrees).

In the meantime, place green beans and chicken stock in a large microwave-safe bowl or dish. Partially cover and cook on high until beans are brightened and crisp-tender. Drain excess stock.

To serve, plate each halibut steak (lemons removed) with a serving of green beans; add a fresh lemon wedge for additional dressing, if desired. Season to taste with sea salt and freshly cracked black pepper.

Note:

Fish dries out easily, especially without the traditional carb-laden coatings and batters. Placing the halibut between layers of lemons helps to keep the fish moist while adding flavor.

Braised Bison with Peppers and Onions

Although still relatively uncommon, bison meat is one of the healthiest out there. The vast majority of bison are raised responsibly, and their meat is similar in taste to beef but very lean. This perfectly seasoned roast pairs well with a simple vegetable sauté.

Serves: 4 to 6

Ingredients

- 1 bison top round or rump roast, approximately 2 to 3 pounds
- 2 tablespoons Simply Organic Steak seasoning blend
- 4 cloves minced fresh garlic, *divided*
- Sea salt and freshly cracked black pepper to taste
- 4 ½ cups beef stock, homemade or purchased (no artificial ingredients), *divided*
- 1 cup sliced button mushrooms
- 2 cups assorted sweet bell peppers (red, green, yellow), sliced into thick strips
- 1 cup sliced yellow onion, separated into rings

Preparation

Preheat your oven to 325 degrees.

Place bison roast in a large, nonstick, oven-safe Dutch oven. Pour in 4 cups broth; add seasoning blend, salt and pepper as desired, and garlic. Cover and cook for 1 hour. Reduce oven temperature to 300, uncover and cook an additional 2 to 2 ½ hours, until roast is cooked through and tender (at least 145 degrees).

Remove roast and allow to rest at least 3 minutes before slicing. Pour pan juices into a small saucepan. Bring to a boil, reduce heat and simmer, uncovered, for approximately 10 minutes or until juices have thickened slightly.

In the meantime, in a large nonstick skillet over medium heat, stir-fry button mushrooms, peppers and onions in remaining ½ cup beef stock (adding more if needed) until crisp-tender.

To serve, slice roast and plate with stir-fried vegetables. Thickened pan juices can be spooned over each serving or placed in a small dipping container at each place setting.

Note:

Due to the low fat content of bison meat, it tends to dry out quickly during dry cooking methods such as roasting. Braising allows the meat to become very tender and absorb all the flavors of the seasonings.

Braised Venison Tenderloin

Venison, or deer meat, can be found in many supermarkets and butcher shops during deer hunting season. Be sure to only purchase from vendors who have their meat fully inspected prior to processing. Venison can have a wild or 'gamey' flavor, which comes from eating a completely natural diet.

Serves: 4

Ingredients

- 1 venison tenderloin (approximately 1 pound)
- 4 cups chicken, beef or vegetable broth, homemade or packaged (no artificial ingredients)
- 2 tablespoons prepared horseradish
- ½ cup chopped red onion
- 2 tablespoons Simply Organic Steak seasoning blend
- 4 cloves garlic, minced, *divided*
- 4 cups baby spinach leaves, washed and dried
- 1 ½ cups sliced button mushrooms
- ½ cup (plus more if needed) chicken stock

Preparation

In a large, nonstick Dutch oven, combine tenderloin, beef stock, horseradish, onion, Simply Organic seasoning blend and 2 cloves minced garlic. Bring to a boil; cover and simmer for 2 to 4 hours or until venison is extremely tender (at least 145 degrees). Remove from Dutch oven and allow to rest at least 3 minutes or until serving.

In the meantime, in a very large nonstick skillet over medium heat, stir-fry spinach in chicken broth until wilted and tender. Add the mushrooms and 2 teaspoons garlic; stir-fry another 3 to 5 minutes or until mushrooms are tender.

To serve, slice the venison into medallions and plate alongside sautéed mushroom-spinach mixture.

If desired, strain the braising liquid and simmer, uncovered, approximately 10 minutes or until reduced and thickened. Serve spooned over each serving of venison or in small cups for dipping.

Note:

In order to remove a great deal of the 'gamey' flavor from venison (useful when feeding children), take care to pull and cut off all visible fat; this is where most of the 'gamey' flavor lies.

Build-Your-Own Cold Salad Bar

Although not technically a recipe, this dinner plan can be a real lifesaver on nights you simply don't feel like cooking. It's also great to set out when entertaining; guests can eat whatever they want while you stick to your Phase Two-approved choices!

Serves: Varies

Ingredients

Thinly sliced deli meats: roast beef, turkey, chicken

Freshly sliced vegetables: broccoli, celery, cucumbers, jalapenos, onions, salad greens, baby spinach, mushrooms, and bell peppers

Accompaniments: Prepared horseradish, mustard, lemon pesto (recipe follows)

Preparation

Arrange all components in a salad-bar fashion or on a tray, and let each diner pick and choose as they like.

Lemon Pesto

In a food processor, process fresh basil, fresh parsley and freshly minced garlic to form a paste. Slowly add a small amount of lemon juice, pulsing after each addition, until the desired consistency is reached. Ingredient amounts can be varied depending on preference.

Greek-Style Burgers with Cucumber Relish

A great, quick-cooking dinner option that's also kid-friendly, these burgers have the fresh flavors of the Mediterranean without unwanted fats and oils!

Serves: 4

Ingredients

- 1 pound lean ground beef, formed into patties
- 1 to 3 tablespoons chicken stock (if needed)
- 3 cups chopped cucumber
- ½ cup chopped fresh parsley
- 2 tablespoons chopped fresh dill
- ½ cup chopped fresh mint leaves
- ½ cup chopped green bell pepper
- ½ fresh lemon
- 4 cups baby spinach, washed and dried

Preparation

In a large nonstick skillet, sauté beef patties until cooked through (at least 160 degrees). Set aside.

In a large bowl, combine cucumbers, parsley, dill, mint and bell pepper. Squeeze lemon over mixture and toss to coat.

To serve, divide spinach leaves among 4 plates. Top each with a beef patty; spoon a generous amount of cucumber relish over each patty. Serve with an additional lemon wedge if desired.

Garlic Roasted Leg of Lamb

Special enough for any celebration but simple enough for a family meal!

Serves: 6

Ingredients

- 1 bone-in leg of lamb (approximately 6 ½ pounds)
- ¼ cup freshly squeezed lemon juice
- 8 cloves fresh garlic, minced
- 3 tablespoons chopped fresh rosemary (or 3 teaspoons dried)
- 1 tablespoon sea salt
- 2 teaspoons freshly cracked black pepper
- ⅓ cup chopped fresh chives
- ⅓ cup chopped fresh rosemary
- ⅓ cup chopped fresh parsley
- 2 cups chopped yellow onions
- 3 cups beef stock (homemade or packaged, no artificial ingredients)
- 4 cups fresh baby spinach, washed and dried
- 1 cup thinly sliced leeks
- ¼ cup beef or chicken stock

Preparation

Preheat oven to 400 degrees.

In a small bowl, combine lemon juice, garlic, 3 tablespoons rosemary, salt and pepper. Pat seasoning mixture over lamb, thoroughly rubbing into the meat. Place a wire rack inside a roasting pan; (continued on next page)

Preparation (continued)

Place lamb on rack and roast for 30 minutes.

Reduce oven heat to 350 degrees; continue roasting until lamb is cooked to desired doneness (at least 145 degrees; see Note). Remove from oven and allow lamb to rest for 10 minutes.

Carefully remove wire rack and place roasting pan onto your stove, covering 2 burners. Add ⅓ cup each chives, rosemary and parsley, the onions and beef stock to pan drippings. Stir to loosen any browned bits from the bottom of the pan. Bring the mixture to a boil; reduce to a simmer and cook, uncovered, until reduced and thickened, at least 10 minutes.

In the meantime, in a very large nonstick skillet, sauté leeks in ¼ cup broth until crisp-tender. Add spinach leaves; stir to combine, cover and remove from heat. Let stand for approximately 5 minutes, or until spinach is slightly wilted.

To serve, slice lamb and plate with spinach-leek mixture. Spoon pan dripping sauce over each serving, or place in individual cups for dipping.

Note:

When testing the internal temperature of bone-in cuts of meat, be careful not to touch the bone with the thermometer. Temperature readings should always be taken from the thickest portion of the meat itself.

Phase Two Snacks

Herbed Deli Slices

Using your oven, transform regular deli meats into deliciously crisped snack options!

Serves: Varies

Ingredients

- Deli-sliced roast beef, turkey or chicken (nitrate-free)
- Simply Organic seasoning blend of your choice

Preparation

Preheat oven to 400 degrees. Lightly sprinkle seasoning blend over deli meat slices. Place on a foil-lined baking sheet and cook, checking every few minutes, approximately 7 to 10 minutes or until lightly browned and crisped. Serve immediately.

Seasoned Tuna

Packaged tuna is an excellent Phase Two snack option, high in protein, highly portable and delicious! Seasoning blends allow you to customize your snack so it doesn't become boring. To keep this option as simple, consider stashing a few small bottles of your favorite blends in your car or your desk at work.

Serves: 1

Ingredients

- 1 pouch (or can) responsibly-caught tuna
- 1 teaspoon (or to taste) Simply Organic seasoning blend of your choice.

Preparation

Pack in a chilled lunch container; open tuna and stir in or sprinkle on seasoning blend just before serving.

Jerky and Eggs for One

Packed with protein and more interesting than a plain hardboiled egg white, this snack gives you more options than bacon and eggs.

Serves: 1

Ingredients

- 2 egg whites
- 1 ounce beef, turkey, buffalo, ostrich or elk jerky (nitrate- and sugar-free), chopped

Preparation

Scramble the egg in a nonstick skillet; sprinkle on chopped jerky when partially set and continue cooking until set and cooked through (160 degrees). Season with sea salt and pepper if desired and serve immediately.

Chapter 3

Phase 3

Carbs, Fruits, Proteins, Veggies & Healthy Fats

<u>Phase Three Breakfasts</u>

Better-Than PB&J with Spinach Scramble

Simple and quick, this two-dish breakfast option gives you all your Phase Three requirements without sacrificing taste or time!

Serves: 1

Ingredients

- 2 slices sprouted-grain bread, toasted
- 2 tablespoons raw almond butter (made with approved oils)
- ¼ cup strawberries
- ⅛ teaspoon Stevia (if desired)
- 1 egg
- 1 to 2 teaspoons almond milk (if desired)
- ½ cup fresh baby spinach leaves
- 1 teaspoon coconut oil.
- Sea salt and freshly cracked black pepper

Preparation

Spread 1 tablespoon almond butter on one side of each slice of toasted bread.

Using a fork, mash strawberries lightly, add Stevia if desired and spoon or spread onto one slice of bread; top with remaining slice and press lightly.

In a small bowl, whisk eggs, adding almond milk if desired.

In a skillet over medium heat, heat 1 teaspoon coconut oil.

Scramble the egg, stirring and lifting until nearly set. Add the spinach leaves; stir to combine and continue cooking until cooked through (160 degrees) and set.

Plate eggs, seasoning to taste with salt and pepper.

Serve alongside almond-strawberry sandwich.

Coconut Pancakes with Rhubarb-Pineapple Sauce

Serve these tropical pancakes with a serving of grains for a complete Phase Three treat!

Serves: 4

Ingredients

- 2 cups chopped rhubarb, fresh or frozen
- 1 cup fresh raspberries, rinsed
- ½ cup water
- ½ cup coconut flour
- ⅛ teaspoon Stevia (optional)
- 1 teaspoon baking soda
- ½ teaspoon sea salt
- 4 eggs
- 1 cup unsweetened coconut milk
- 2 teaspoons real vanilla extract
- Coconut oil, for frying

Preparation

In a small saucepan over medium heat, combine rhubarb, raspberries and water. Smash lightly with a fork. Simmer, stirring frequently to prevent burning, until mixture has reduced to the consistency of a sauce. Taste and add Stevia if desired; set aside.

Heat a large nonstick skillet or nonstick griddle over medium-low heat. (Continued on next page)

Preparation (continued)

In a bowl, whisk together the eggs, coconut milk, vanilla and Stevia (if desired) until well combined and slightly frothy. With a hand whisk, this should take approximately 2 minutes; with an electric mixer it should take between 30 seconds to 1 minute. In another bowl, combine the coconut flour, baking soda and salt; whisking to incorporate

Add the wet mixture to the dry mixture, in portions if necessary, stirring well to fully combine. Batter will be thick; if you prefer a thinner pancake, add more almond milk, 1 teaspoon at a time, until desired consistency is reached.

When griddle or pan is heated, grease with coconut oil and place approximately 2 tablespoons of batter per pancake onto griddle. For thicker batters, you may want to press the batter down to create a pancake approximately 2 to 3 inches in diameter.

Cook for 3 to 4 minutes, or until the tops begin to dry out and bottoms are golden brown. Flip and cook another 3 to 4 minutes, or until fully cooked through. Serve topped with rhubarb-raspberry sauce, alongside a sprouted-grain bagel or other grain option.

Note:

Rhubarb, in the Fast Metabolism book, is listed under both vegetables and fruits, making it a versatile option.

Southwest Spiced Frittata

Great for big family breakfasts, this deliciously savory frittata becomes a complete Phase Three breakfast when served alongside the fresh fruit and grain of your choice!

Serves: 6

Ingredients

- ¼ pound chicken or turkey sausage, nitrate-free, casings removed (choose a neutral flavor)
- 1 cup firmly packed baby spinach leaves
- 1 ½ cups chopped Roma tomatoes
- ½ cup chopped avocado
- ¼ cup scallions, sliced
- 7 eggs
- 1 teaspoon chili powder
- ¼ teaspoon cumin
- ⅛ teaspoon red pepper flakes

Preparation

Preheat oven to 375.

Cook and crumble the sausage in a large, nonstick, oven-proof skillet until fully cooked and no pink remains. Remove and set on paper towels to drain.

In the same skillet, sauté spinach until it wilts; approximately 3 minutes. Stir in tomatoes, avocado and scallions. Return the cooked sausage to pan.

In a bowl, whisk eggs, chili powder, cumin and red pepper flakes. Add mixture to vegetable-sausage mixture in skillet; stir to combine. Place in oven and cook for 25 to 30 minutes or until eggs are cooked through and set (160 degrees). Cut into wedges and serve alongside fresh fruit (see Note).

Note:

Blueberries, blackberries, cherries, grapefruit halves, peaches, plums and raspberries would all make deliciously fresh accompaniments to this frittata. Avocados, though technically a fruit, are counted as a vegetable in this diet's guidelines.

For a simple serving of grain, toast slices of sprouted-grain bread or bagels. For heartier appetites, a serving of steel-cut oats topped with fruit would also be acceptable.

Berry Blast Oatmeal

With its delicious triple-berry flavor burst and paired with a simple celery-almond butter, this Phase Three breakfast is a great way to start off chilly mornings!

Serves: 1

Ingredients

- ¾ cup old-fashioned oats (not quick-cooking)
- 1 ½ cups water or almond milk (unsweetened)
- Dash of sea salt (optional)
- 1 cup combined blueberries, raspberries and strawberries, rinsed and hulled
- 2 tablespoons water
- ⅛ teaspoon Stevia (optional)
- 1 large stalk celery, cut into 2-inch slices
- 2 tablespoons raw almond butter (prepared with approved oils)

Preparation

In a saucepan over medium heat, combine oats, water (or almond milk) and salt if desired. Bring to a boil, reduce heat and simmer, uncovered, for approximately 5 minutes or until desired consistency is reached.

In the meantime, lightly mash berries and place in a small saucepan with 2 tablespoons water. Cook over low heat, stirring frequently, until reduced and syrupy. Taste and add Stevia if desired.

Spread each celery stick with almond butter. Top the oatmeal with berry mixture and serve alongside celery sticks.

Note:

If you prefer a chewier texture to your oatmeal, boil the water (or almond milk) and salt first, then add oats; continue as directed.

To save time, you may skip the reducing step and simply top your oatmeal with fresh berries and a sprinkling of Stevia.

Almond Raspberry Smoothies

When served alongside almond-buttered vegetables and toast, these smoothies are a great way to get the whole family off to a healthy, quick start!

Serves: 4

Ingredients

2 cups unsweetened almond milk

12 ounces (1 ¾ cups) frozen raspberries (do not thaw)

1 cup crushed or cubed ice

½ teaspoon real vanilla extract

2 cups baby carrots and fresh celery sticks

4 slices sprouted-grain bread, toasted

1 cup almond butter

Preparation

In a blender, combine the almond milk, frozen raspberries, ice and vanilla until smooth. Pour into glasses.

Spread the carrots and celery with half of the almond butter, or serve it alongside for dipping. Spread the remaining almond butter on toasted bread slices.

Coconut Carob Oatmeal with Pecans

Delicious and filling, the generous amount of pecans in this quick recipe serves as both your protein and healthy fats!

Serves: 1

Ingredients

- ¾ cup old-fashioned oats (not quick-cooking)
- 1 ½ cups water or unsweetened almond milk
- ⅛ teaspoon sea salt (optional)
- ¼ cup unsweetened shredded coconut
- ½ cup raw pecan halves or pieces
- ¼ cup sliced sweet cherries, pitted
- 2 tablespoons carob chips

Preparation

Place the oats, water (or almond milk) and salt if desired in a saucepan; bring to a boil. Reduce heat and simmer for 5 minutes or until desired consistency is reached. Top with pecans, cherries, coconut and carob chips to serve.

Note:

Carob chips, a healthy alternative to chocolate which tastes remarkably similar, can be found in health food stores and in the natural-products section of most large supermarkets.

Bacon-Jalapeno Sweet Potato Hash

Boldly flavored and great for relaxed mornings, this simple hash provides your vegetable and fat/protein requirements. Add a fresh fruit and grain serving to complete this savory Phase Three breakfast!

Serves: 4

Ingredients

- 4 strips turkey bacon, nitrate-free, chopped
- 3 tablespoons organic olive oil
- 1 pound sweet potatoes, peeled and diced into ¼ inch pieces
- ½ cup chopped yellow onion
- 2 cloves fresh garlic, minced
- 1 tablespoon chopped fresh jalapeno peppers (see Note)
- 1 ½ teaspoons chili powder
- ½ teaspoon cumin
- Sea salt and freshly cracked black pepper to taste
- ¼ cup fresh cilantro, chopped, for garnish

Preparation

Place the bacon and olive oil in a large skillet and heat over medium-high heat. When you can hear the bacon sizzling, add the sweet potatoes. Working with a spatula, spread the sweet potatoes into a single layer to ensure even cooking.

Cook the bacon and potatoes, without stirring, for approximately 5 minutes or until the bottom is nicely browned. Toss and stir; cook for another 3 to 5 minutes. Repeat as necessary until the potatoes are cooked through and uniformly browned, and the bacon is crisp.

Add the onion, garlic, jalapeno, chili powder, cumin, salt and pepper to the skillet; toss and cook for 1 to 2 minutes longer or until heated through and flavors have combined. Divide mixture between 4 plates, garnish with cilantro if desired and serve alongside a fruit and grain of your choice.

Note:

Be very careful when handling jalapenos, as their oils can severely burn your eyes.

Quick Sausage Sandwiches with Almond-Butter Berries

These simple sandwiches are a snap to prepare, especially if you pre-cook and freeze the sausage patties! Round out your Phase Three breakfast with deliciously creamy almond butter-topped berries for a decadent option that tastes like dessert!

Serves: 4

Ingredients

- ¾ to 1 pound chicken or turkey breakfast sausage (nitrate free, casings removed)
- 8 slices sprouted grain bread OR 4 sprouted-grain bagels, toasted
- 1 cup baby spinach leaves, washed and dried
- ½ cup chopped avocado
- 1 cup mixed berries (blueberries, blackberries, strawberries or cherries)
- ¾ cup raw almond butter (prepared with approved oils)
- 1 to 2 tablespoons unsweetened almond milk

Preparation

Shape the sausage into 4 patties. In a large skillet, cook over medium heat until golden brown and cooked through and, if using uncooked sausage, no pink remains (165 degrees).

Assemble the sandwiches by spreading one side of all bread or bagel slices with avocado; place a sausage patty on avocado and top with spinach. Cover with remaining bread slices and press down lightly.

In a small bowl, whisk together almond butter and almond milk until a creamy consistency is reached. Divide berries between 4 small bowls; top with almond butter sauce.

Italian Scrambled Eggs

Scrambled eggs have been a breakfast favorite for many years, and with good reason — they're healthy, amazingly versatile and extremely easy! This delicious version captures the tastes of Italy with tomatoes and fresh herbs. Serve over a toasted slice of bread with a side of fresh fruit to round out your Phase Three breakfast!

Serves: 4

Ingredients

- 12 eggs
- 3 tablespoons water
- 1 to 2 teaspoons olive oil
- 3 cloves fresh garlic, minced
- 2 cups chopped Roma tomatoes, drained (see Note)
- ¼ cup chopped fresh basil
- ¼ cup chopped fresh oregano OR 1 tablespoon dried
- 4 slices sprouted-grain bread, toasted
- Fresh fruit of your choice (see Note)

Preparation

In a large bowl, whisk eggs and water.

Heat the olive oil in a large nonstick skillet over medium heat. Add the eggs; cook and stir until nearly set.

Add the tomatoes, basil and oregano; continue cooking and stirring until completely set and cooked through (160 degrees).

Serve eggs over toasts slices, alongside fresh fruit.

Note:

While it's a matter of personal tastes, many people find that raw tomatoes can make egg dishes too watery. You can easily drain chopped tomatoes by placing them on a paper-towel-covered plate for 5 minutes; this will draw out excess moisture and deliver a fluffy, delicious egg dish.

Smoked Salmon Bagel with Avocado and Onion

A delicious twist on traditional dairy- and carb-heavy smoked salmon breakfasts; this healthier and fresher-tasting version combines your fat/protein, grain and vegetable servings into one delicious sandwich! Pair with the fresh fruit of your choice to make this a quick and complete Phase Three breakfast!

Serves: 1

Ingredients

- 1 ounce good-quality smoked salmon (nitrate-free)
- 1 sprouted-grain bagel, split and toasted
- ½ cup cubed avocado
- 1 to 2 very thin slices red onion

Preparation

Fruit options: Mixed berries, halved grapefruit or peaches would all provide a deliciously refreshing option

In a bowl, lightly mash avocado cubes; spread on both bagel halves. On one half, layer smoked salmon and red onion, top with remaining bagel half and serve alongside fruit of choice.

Phase Three Lunches

Plum-Turkey Wraps

A fun and unique take on turkey salad, these refreshing wraps combine all components of your Phase Three lunch in one dish!

Serves: 4

Ingredients

- 1 ½ cups shredded, cooked turkey (see Note)
- 1 cup chopped fresh plums
- ½ cup chopped fresh celery
- ½ cup sliced scallions
- ½ cup chopped fresh parsley
- ¼ cup chopped raw walnuts
- ¾ cup safflower mayonnaise
- Sea salt and freshly cracked black pepper to taste
- 4 (or more as needed) leaves lettuce (Romaine, Bibb or Boston)

Preparation

Combine turkey, plums, celery, scallions, parsley, walnuts and mayonnaise in a bowl; toss to coat. Season to taste with salt and pepper.

To serve, spoon salad onto lettuce leaves; serve open or roll up to form sandwiches.

Tuscan Style Chicken Soup

Ideal for weeknight dinners, this quick soup features the bright flavors of the Mediterranean without unwanted carbs! Pair with the Phase Three fruit of your choice.

Serves: 4

Ingredients

- 1 tablespoon extra-virgin olive oil
- 1 pound uncooked chicken strips, sliced into 2-inch pieces (see Note)
- ¾ cup sliced red onion
- 2 teaspoons fresh minced garlic
- 1 can (28 ounces) diced tomatoes, undrained (no sugar added)
- 1 cup sliced carrots
- 3 ½ cups chicken stock (homemade or packaged, no artificial ingredients
- 1 tablespoon Simply Organic Italian seasoning blend
- 1 ½ cups sliced celery
- ¼ cup fresh sliced basil
- ¼ cup fresh chopped oregano

Preparation

In a large nonstick skillet over medium heat, heat the olive oil; add chicken pieces, onion and garlic. Cook and stir for approximately 5 to 7 minutes or until chicken is browned and onion and garlic are fragrant but not burned.

Add the tomatoes, carrots, chicken stock and Italian seasoning. Bring to a boil; reduce heat and simmer, uncovered, 10 minutes. Add the celery; bring to boiling again, reduce heat and simmer an additional 3 to 5 minutes or until vegetables are tender and chicken is cooked through (160 degrees).

Garnish individual bowls with fresh herbs to serve.

Note:

In many supermarkets, you can find pre-sliced chicken pieces. These time-savers are usually labeled 'stir fry' cuts.

Potential Fruit pairings: Blueberries, blackberries, cherries, raspberries, grapefruit, plums, peaches

Spanish Burger Wraps with Olive Relish

A delicious twist on traditional burgers, these savory wraps capture the flavors of Spain and get an added kick from hot sauce. When preparing for children, consider leaving out the hot sauce or offering it on the side. Pair these burgers with fruit to complete your Phase Three lunch.

Serves: 4

Ingredients

Relish:

- ⅓ cup chopped and seeded Roma tomatoes
- ⅓ cup chopped organic cucumber
- ½ cup olives, any type
- 2 tablespoons finely chopped radishes
- 2 tablespoons red or yellow onion, finely chopped
- ⅛ teaspoon Tabasco or other hot-pepper sauce

Burgers:

- 1 egg (or refrigerated, pasteurized liquid eggs)
- ¼ cup fresh parsley, chopped
- ½ teaspoon dried thyme OR 1 ½ teaspoons fresh, chopped
- 1 pound lean ground beef OR buffalo meat
- 1 teaspoon olive oil (optional)
- 4 large leaves (or more if needed) lettuce, spinach or kale, washed thoroughly and dried

Preparation

In a small bowl, combine relish ingredients; place in refrigerator and chill until serving.

In a larger bowl, combine egg, parsley, thyme and ground meat. Shape into 4 patties. In a large nonstick skillet over medium heat, cook the burgers (in olive oil if desired) approximately 6 minutes per side, or until cooked through (160 degrees) and no pink remains.

To assemble, place a burger patty on a lettuce leaf and spoon relish over top. Roll up into a sandwich and serve immediately, alongside fresh fruit.

Rice and Sesame Stuffed Portobellos

Bursting with Asian flavors, these huge mushroom caps are filled with a brown rice-sesame filling to satisfy your vegetable and fat/protein requirements; pair them with a serving of fresh fruit to round out your Phase Three lunch!

Serves: 4

Ingredients

- ¾ cup uncooked brown rice
- 1 ½ cups water or chicken stock
- 4 large (6 inch) Portobello mushroom caps, washed
- 1 tablespoon plus 1 teaspoon organic light-flavored olive oil, *divided*
- 1 cup shredded cooked chicken
- 1 cup shredded cabbage
- 1 cup shredded carrots
- ¼ cup sliced scallions
- 1 tablespoon freshly grated ginger
- 1 clove fresh garlic, minced
- 3 teaspoons toasted sesame oil
- 4 teaspoons raw sesame seeds

Preparation

Preheat oven to 400 degrees. In a saucepan, combine rice with water or stock. Bring to a boil; cover, reduce heat and simmer until rice is done, approximately 45 to 50 minutes.

In the meantime, lightly grease a large, flat baking sheet with 1 teaspoon olive oil. Place the mushroom caps onto the baking sheet, round sides up. Bake approximately 5 minutes or until slightly tender and lightly browned.

In a large nonstick skillet over medium heat, heat the remaining 1 tablespoon olive oil. Add the chicken and stir-fry 3 to 4 minutes or until thoroughly heated through. Add the cabbage, carrots, scallions, ginger and garlic; stir-fry approximately 2 to 3 minutes. Stir in rice and toasted sesame oil; cook and stir approximately another minute, or until mixture is heated through, vegetables are tender and cabbage is wilted.

To serve, place each Portobello cap on a plate and spoon rice-cabbage mixture on top. Sprinkle with sesame seeds and serve alongside the fruit of your choice (see Note).

Note:

Phase Three fruit options include blueberries, blackberries, strawberries, cherries, grapefruit, plums and peaches.

Chicken Guacamole Salad

Combining everybody's favorite party dip with healthy, lean protein, this quick-to-assemble salad is great for using up leftover chicken and combines all your Phase Three lunch requirements in a single dish!

Serves: 6

Ingredients

- 1 ½ cup cooked chicken, cubed or shredded
- 2 cups chopped and seeded Roma tomatoes
- 1 cup chopped bell pepper, any color
- 1 (15 ounce) can black beans, rinsed and drained
- 2 fresh jalapeno peppers, seeded and minced
- ¼ cup red onion, minced
- 2 slightly under-ripe peaches, peeled and chopped
- ¼ cup freshly squeezed lime juice
- 1 teaspoon freshly grated lime zest
- ¼ cup organic, extra-virgin olive oil
- 1 teaspoon chili powder
- ¼ cup fresh cilantro, chopped
- 2 ½ cups cubed avocado (approximately 2 whole)
- Sea salt and freshly cracked black pepper to taste

Preparation

Combine chicken, tomatoes, peppers, beans, jalapenos, onion and peaches in a large serving bowl. In a small bowl, stir together lime juice, lime zest, olive oil, chili powder and cilantro. Pour over salad and toss to combine.

Gently stir in avocados, being careful not to crush or mash. Toss gently to coat, season as desired with salt and pepper and serve immediately.

Chicken Salad with Roasted Carrots and Peaches

Fulfilling all of your Phase Three requirements in a single dish, this brightly-flavored salad pairs the rich, roasted flavor of carrots with the refreshing sweetness of fresh peaches!

Serves: 4

Ingredients

- 2 cups carrots, peeled and sliced ½ inch thick
- 3 tablespoons organic extra-virgin olive oil, *divided*
- ½ teaspoon sea salt
- ¼ teaspoon freshly cracked black pepper
- 3 cups cooked chicken, shredded
- Additional sea salt and freshly cracked black pepper, as desired
- ¼ cup chopped green onions
- 2 cups baby spinach OR mixed salad greens, washed and dried
- 1 ½ cups fresh peaches, peeled and cubed
- 1 ½ tablespoons cider vinegar
- 1 clove garlic, minced
- 2 tablespoons chopped raw pecans

Preparation

Preheat oven to 325 degrees. On a large, nonstick, rimmed baking sheet, combine carrots, 1 tablespoon olive oil, salt and pepper. Roast, stirring occasionally, until carrots are tender and lightly golden brown, approximately 25 minutes.

Approximately 5 to 6 minutes before carrots are done, spread chicken onto another baking sheet and toss with 1 tablespoon olive oil, green onions and additional salt and pepper if desired. Place in oven and cook until carrots are done or until chicken is safely heated through (160 degrees).

In a bowl, combine greens, peaches, cider vinegar and remaining 1 tablespoon olive oil. Toss to combine. To serve, divide greens between 4 plates. Top with chicken and roasted carrots, sprinkle with chopped pecans and serve immediately.

Tropical Cajun Salad

Combining the bold flavors of Cajun and Caribbean cuisine, this salad combines all your Phase Three requirements into a boldly-seasoned dish that's perfect for warm-weather entertaining!

Serves: 4

Ingredients

- 1 pound boneless skinless chicken breast strips, approximately ½ inch thick
- 2 tablespoons Simply Organic Jambalaya seasoning blend
- 1 tablespoon extra-virgin olive oil
- ½ cup fresh raspberries
- 2 tablespoons balsamic vinegar
- 2 cups baby spinach leaves, washed and drained
- 2 cups baby arugula, washed and drained
- 1 cup chopped and peeled fresh peaches
- ¾ cup red or yellow onion, chopped
- ½ cup green bell pepper, chopped

Preparation

Coat the chicken strips with Jambalaya seasoning. Heat the olive oil in a large nonstick skillet, add chicken and cook and stir for approximately 8 to 11 minutes or until no pink remains (160 degrees). Drain on paper towels to remove excess oil.

In a food processor, process raspberries and vinegar until dressing consistency is achieved.

Toss salad greens, peaches, onion and bell pepper in a large bowl. Divide between 4 plates, top with seasoned chicken and drizzle with raspberry vinaigrette.

Two-Bean Chicken Stew

Hearty and satisfying, this updated twist on chicken stew is loaded with lean protein and vegetables. Pair it with a simple fruit to complete your Phase Three lunch!

Serves: 6

Ingredients

- 2 tablespoons organic extra-virgin olive oil, *divided*
- 1 cup chopped fresh green bell pepper
- ¾ cup chopped red onion
- 1 pound boneless, skinless chicken breasts or thighs, cut into bite-size pieces
- 2 cups chicken stock, homemade or purchased, no artificial ingredients
- ½ teaspoon organic arrowroot powder
- 2 tablespoons tomato paste, no sugar added
- 1 tablespoon fresh thyme, chopped OR 1 teaspoon dried
- Few dashes hot-pepper sauce
- Sea salt and freshly cracked black pepper, as desired
- 2 cloves fresh garlic, minced
- 1 can (15 ounces) butter beans, rinsed and drained
- 1 package (10 ounces) frozen lima beans

Preparation

In a large, nonstick stockpot over medium heat, heat 1 tablespoon olive oil. Add the green pepper and onion; cook and stir approximately 5 minutes or until onion is fragrant but not browned.

Add the chicken and remaining tablespoon olive oil; cook, stirring occasionally, until chicken has browned on all sides, approximately 2 to 4 minutes. Add the broth and arrowroot powder; bring to a boil and cook until stew has thickened slightly, approximately 1 to 2 minutes.

Add the tomato paste, thyme, hot-pepper sauce, garlic, butter beans and lima beans. Bring back to a boil; reduce heat and simmer, covered, for 30 minutes. Season to taste with salt and pepper and serve immediately.

Note:

For a quick lunch on the go, this stew can be prepared the night before, transferred into smaller containers and refrigerated or frozen. In the morning, heat up a serving and place in an insulated thermos, or pack a frozen portion to thaw in the microwave at work.

Chilling or freezing large amounts of any hot food should be done in small containers; they cool off much more quickly and avoid heating up your refrigerator or freezer.

BLT Avocado Burger Wraps

Taking the classic flavors of a traditionally light BLT sandwich and making them extra-hearty, these burgers are great for cookouts! Technically the avocado on these burgers can count as a fruit, but you may also have a small serving of fresh fruit on the side if you wish.

Serves: 4

Ingredients

- 8 slices turkey bacon (nitrate-free), crisply cooked and drained on paper towels
- 1 pound lean ground beef or buffalo meat, shaped into patties
- ¼ teaspoon hot-pepper sauce
- 1 ½ teaspoons chopped fresh thyme OR ¼ teaspoon dried
- 2 large tomatoes, sliced
- 1 red onion, sliced thin
- 1 large avocado, sliced
- 4 (or more as needed) large leaves Boston lettuce

Preparation

In a large nonstick skillet over medium heat, cook the burger patties for approximately 4 to 5 minutes, turn, and cook another 3 to 4 minutes, or until no pink remains and patties are cooked through (165 degrees).

To assemble, place a burger patty in the middle of each lettuce leaf. Add tomato, avocado and onion slices; fold or roll into a hand-held 'pocket' and serve immediately with a fresh fruit accompaniment.

Fruited Turkey Salad with Cashews

Yet another way to get all your Phase Three requirements in a single dish, this refreshing yet satisfying salad is also ideal for using up leftover turkey!

Serves: 4

Ingredients

- 2 cups cooked turkey, shredded or chopped
- 2 cups sliced celery
- 2 tablespoons chopped green onions
- 2 small, sweet oranges, peeled, segmented, each segment cut in half
- 1 tablespoon freshly grated ginger
- 1 cup raw cashews
- ½ cup safflower mayonnaise
- 4 cups baby spinach, baby arugula or mixed salad greens, washed and dried

Preparation

In a large bowl, combine turkey, celery, green onions, oranges, ginger and cashews. Stir in mayonnaise, tossing to coat evenly. Divide salad greens between 4 plates, top with turkey salad and serve. Refrigerate any leftovers immediately.

Phase Three Dinners

Garlic Roasted Beef with Tomato Relish

Hearty, flavorful and satisfying, this garlic-infused beef roast pairs beautifully with the broiled-tomato and onion relish. If you wish to include an optional serving of grains, wild rice would go nicely with this Phase Three dinner.

Serves: 4 to 6

Ingredients

- 1 beef or buffalo roast (approximately 2 ½ to 2 ¾ pounds), fat trimmed
- 3 cloves fresh garlic, sliced into slivers
- ½ teaspoon dried basil, crushed
- ½ teaspoon dried rosemary, crushed
- 4 tablespoons organic, extra-virgin olive oil, *divided*
- 3 large Roma tomatoes, thickly sliced
- 1 small red onion, sliced
- 1 tablespoon balsamic vinegar
- ¼ cup fresh basil leaves, chopped or sliced
- Sea salt and freshly cracked black pepper

Preparation

Preheat your broiler.

On a nonstick, rimmed baking sheet, combine tomatoes and onion with olive oil; toss to coat. Drizzle on balsamic vinegar; stir to combine.

Broil approximately 4 inches from the heat until tomatoes and onions begin to brown and caramelize, approximately 5 minutes (broiling times vary widely depending on thickness of slices, distance from heat and other factors, so watch carefully).

Remove broiled vegetables, drain on paper towels and chill until serving.

Preheat oven to 400 degrees.

Rub your roast with 2 tablespoons olive oil; rub generously with salt and pepper. In a small bowl, combine garlic slivers and crushed herbs. Cut small slits into the roast; insert an herb-coated garlic sliver into each slit.

Place roast on a wire rack in a roasting pan; roast for 45 minutes to 1 hour, 30 minutes, depending on desired doneness (at least 145 degrees). Remove and allow the roast to rest at least 15 minutes before slicing.

To serve, plate several slices roast beef; top with chilled tomato-onion relish and garnish with fresh basil.

Chicken Quinoa Casserole

A delicious and much healthier alternative to most traditional casseroles, this Phase Three dinner includes your optional grain serving, making it a true one-dish-meal!

Serves: 4 to 6

Ingredients

- 1 ¾ cups chicken stock, homemade or packaged (no artificial ingredients)
- ¾ cup uncooked quinoa
- 3 tablespoons olive oil, *divided*
- 2 small yellow straight-neck squash, sliced (also called yellow summer squash)
- ½ cup chopped fresh scallions
- 2 tablespoons chopped fresh basil
- 1 tablespoon chopped fresh rosemary
- 2 tablespoons chopped fresh oregano
- 2 cloves garlic, minced
- 2 cups cooked shredded chicken
- ¼ cup liquid pasteurized eggs
- Sea salt and freshly cracked black pepper as desired

Preparation

Preheat oven to 400 degrees.

In a saucepan, combine stock and quinoa. Bring to a boil; reduce heat and simmer until all liquid is absorbed.

In a very large nonstick skillet, heat 1 tablespoon olive oil. Add the squash, scallions, basil, rosemary, oregano and garlic; sauté approximately 3 to 5 minutes or until squash is tender.

Combine cooked quinoa, squash mixture, chicken and pasteurized egg in a large bowl; stir to thoroughly incorporate. Grease an 8-inch baking dish with remaining tablespoon olive oil; spoon casserole mixture into dish and bake for approximately 30 minutes or until golden brown and heated through. Serve immediately.

Spicy Taco Wraps

This family-favorite dinner idea can easily be modified if you want to incorporate grains. Simply swap out the lettuce wraps for sprouted-grain tortillas!

Serves: 4

Ingredients

- 1 beef or buffalo flank steak (approximately 1 ½ to 1 ¾ pounds), fat trimmed
- 1 tablespoon Simply Organic Southwest Taco seasoning blend
- 1 tablespoon extra-virgin olive oil
- 2 cups chopped Roma tomatoes
- 1 large avocado, cubed
- ½ cup chopped fresh cilantro
- 3 cloves garlic, minced
- ⅓ cup green onions, chopped
- 1 fresh jalapeno pepper, seeded and chopped
- 1 teaspoon chili powder
- ½ teaspoon cumin
- ¼ cup freshly squeezed lime juice
- 4 (or more as needed) large leaves Bibb or Romaine lettuce
- Lime wedges (optional)

Preparation

Slice the steak, against the grain, into strips. In a large nonstick skillet over medium heat, combine steak, taco seasoning and olive oil. Cook the steak until browned and no pink remains (145 degrees), approximately 10 minutes.

In the meantime, combine tomatoes, avocado, cilantro, garlic, green onions, jalapeno, chili powder and lime juice in a bowl. Add the lime juice, a tablespoon at a time, until all ingredients are dressed and coated. Toss a few times to thoroughly combine, being careful not to crush or mash avocado.

To assemble, place a portion of steak strips and a portion of tomato-avocado mixture onto each lettuce leaf; roll or fold up to form a taco or sandwich. Serve immediately, with extra lime wedges, if desired, for garnish.

Greek Style Chicken with Tomato-Olive Relish

The flavors of the Mediterranean are bold in this surprisingly simple chicken dish – serve alongside a small portion of dill-and-mint-seasoned quinoa if desired.

Serves: 4

Ingredients

- 4 boneless, skinless chicken breasts
- 4 tablespoons organic extra-virgin olive oil, *divided*
- Sea salt and freshly cracked black pepper, as desired
- 2 small Roma tomatoes, seeded and chopped
- ⅓ cup Kalamata olives, chopped and drained on paper towels
- ⅓ cup chopped scallions
- 1 ½ teaspoons chopped fresh oregano OR ½ teaspoon dried
- ¼ cup chopped fresh dill
- ¼ cup chopped fresh mint leaves
- 4 cups baby spinach leaves
- 2 tablespoons balsamic vinegar

Preparation

Heat a nonstick skillet or grill pan over medium heat. Add 1 tablespoon olive oil; place the chicken in pan and season with salt and pepper. Cook, turning once, approximately 8 to 10 minutes or until juices run clear and no pink remains (170 degrees).

In the meantime, in a bowl, combine tomatoes, olives, scallions, oregano, dill, mint and 1 tablespoon olive oil; toss to coat.

To serve, divide spinach between 4 plates; dress as desired with remaining olive oil, balsamic vinegar and salt and pepper if desired. Place a chicken breast onto each plate; spoon tomato-olive relish over each chicken breast. Serve immediately.

Baked Eggplant Chicken with Crumb Topping

If you'd rather not have grains with this Phase Three dinner, simply leave out the bread-crumb topping and bake until heated through!

Serves: 4 to 6

Ingredients

- 4 boneless, skinless chicken breasts
- 1 eggplant (approximately 1 ½ pounds), peeled and sliced ¼ inch thick
- 4 large Roma tomatoes, thickly sliced
- ⅓ cup green or black olives, chopped
- ½ teaspoon crushed red pepper flakes
- ¼ cup plus 2 tablespoons chopped fresh basil, *divided*
- 1 cup day-old sprouted-grain breadcrumbs
- Organic extra-virgin olive oil, sea salt and freshly cracked black pepper as needed

Preparation

Preheat oven to 450 degrees. On two separate burners over medium heat, heat a nonstick skillet and a nonstick grill pan.

Brush eggplant and tomato slices with olive oil and season with salt and pepper. Grill, turning once, approximately 1 to 2 minutes or until slightly charred but not burned.

In the skillet, heat approximately 1 tablespoon olive oil; add chicken breasts and cook approximately 8 to 10 minutes, turning once, until cooked through (160 degrees) and no pink remains.

In a bowl, toss bread crumbs with approximately 2 tablespoons olive oil.

Brush an 8 or 9-inch baking dish with olive oil. Combine olives and red pepper flakes. Place half of the eggplant slices in baking dish, overlapping if necessary.

Top with chicken breasts. Top the chicken breasts with olive mixture, tomatoes and remaining eggplant slices. Sprinkle bread crumbs over all. Bake for 12 to 15 minutes or until heated through and bread crumbs are crisped and golden. Serve immediately, alongside a green salad if desired.

Sautéed Shrimp with Lime Salsa

Bright, fresh and ideal for cookouts, this light Phase Three dinner can be rounded out with some crisped sprouted-grain tortillas, if desired.

Serves: 4

Ingredients

- 12 large or jumbo-sized shrimp
- 2 tablespoons freshly squeezed lemon or lime juice
- ½ cup organic, extra-virgin olive oil, *divided*
- 2 fresh limes, peeled, segmented, membranes removed
- 2 Roma tomatoes, chopped
- 5 medium-sized radishes, red or white, chopped
- 1 cup red or yellow onion, chopped
- 1 tablespoon chili powder
- 1 teaspoon cumin
- ½ cup fresh cilantro, chopped

Preparation

In a large nonstick skillet over medium heat, sauté shrimp in ¼ cup olive oil and lemon juice until they turn pink, approximately 5 to 8 minutes (cooking times will vary depending on size of shrimp).

In the meantime, combine remaining ¼ cup olive oil, lime segments, tomatoes, radishes, onion, chili powder, cumin and cilantro. Toss to thoroughly combine.

To serve, divide shrimp between 4 plates; spoon salsa over each portion and serve immediately.

Salmon with Vegetable-Herb Brown Rice

Quick to prepare and light yet satisfying, this Phase Three dinner option includes your optional grain serving.

Serves: 4

Ingredients

- 1 cup uncooked brown rice
- 2 ¼ cups chicken stock
- 1 teaspoon dried dill, crushed
- 2 halibut fillets (8 ounces each), cut in half
- 1 to 2 tablespoons organic, extra-virgin olive oil
- 2 teaspoons Simply Organic Lemon Pepper seasoning blend
- 1 cup fresh carrots, sliced
- 1 cup fresh green beans, trimmed
- 3 tablespoons safflower mayonnaise
- 1 tablespoon Dijon mustard
- 2 tablespoons fresh dill, chopped, *divided*
- Additional fresh dill, for garnish, optional

Preparation

In a saucepan, combine brown rice, chicken stock and crushed dill. Bring to a boil; reduce heat and simmer, covered, until rice is cooked, approximately 35 to 50 minutes.

In the meantime, heat olive oil in large, nonstick skillet over medium heat. Season the halibut fillets with lemon pepper seasoning; place in pan and cook, turning once, approximately 8 to 15 minutes or until opaque and fish flakes easily with a fork (145 degrees).

In a small bowl, whisk together safflower mayonnaise, Dijon mustard and fresh dill.

In a microwave-safe dish, combine carrots, green beans and approximately ¼ cup water. Partially cover and cook on high power until vegetables are steamed and crisp-tender.

Toss steamed vegetables, additional chopped dill and herbed rice; divide mixture between 4 plates. Top each serving with a half-fillet of halibut; spoon herbed mustard sauce over top or serve in small individual containers for dipping. Serve additional sprigs of fresh dill as a garnish, if desired.

Olive-Grilled Salmon with Sautéed Vegetables

Fresh and ideal for warm-weather dinners, this Phase Three option does not include a grain. If you like, a small serving of wild rice or herbed brown rice would pair beautifully with this flavorful, heart-healthy fish!

Serves: 4

Ingredients

4 (6 ounce) salmon fillets

- ½ cup plus 1 tablespoon organic, extra-virgin olive oil, *divided*
- ¼ cup red wine or balsamic vinegar
- ½ cup green olives, chopped fine
- ½ teaspoon chili powder
- 2 cloves fresh garlic, minced
- 1 tablespoon grainy brown mustard
- 2 cups fresh green beans, trimmed
- 1 cup red onion, sliced
- 1 cup sliced mushrooms
- Sea salt and freshly cracked black pepper to taste

Preparation

In a heavy-duty plastic freezer bag, combine salmon fillets, ½ cup olive oil, vinegar, olives, chili powder, garlic and brown mustard. Seal, turn several times to coat, and place on a drip-proof dish to marinate for approximately 20 minutes.

In the meantime, heat remaining tablespoon olive oil in a nonstick skillet over medium heat.

Add the green beans, onions and mushrooms; sauté for approximately 5 to 7 minutes or until green beans are crisp-tender and mushrooms are lightly browned. Season to taste with salt and pepper.

While vegetables are cooking, place a grill pan on stove burner over high heat, or preheat barbeque grill to high. Remove salmon from marinade and lightly season with salt and black pepper to taste. Grill to desired result, usually 3 to 4 minutes.

To serve, plate each portion of salmon alongside a portion of green bean mixture. Serve immediately, with a small serving of grain if desired.

Garlicky Bison-Tomato Sauce over Barley

While this hearty sauce resembles a traditional pasta sauce, it is much thicker and closer to a stew in consistency. If you don't want to include a grain with this Phase Three dinner, simply enjoy the stew-like sauce with a fork, alongside a green salad!

Serves: 4

Ingredients

- 1 ½ pounds buffalo stew meat (see Note)
- 1 large red onion, chopped
- 4 cloves fresh garlic, minced
- 2 tablespoons organic, extra-virgin olive oil
- 1 (28 ounce) can diced tomatoes, no sugar added, undrained
- 1 can (6 ounces) tomato paste, no sugar added
- ½ cup chicken or beef stock
- 1 can (15 ounces) cannellini beans, rinsed and drained
- 2 teaspoons dried basil, crushed
- 1 teaspoon sea salt
- 1 tablespoon Simply Organic Italian seasoning blend
- ½ teaspoon freshly cracked black pepper
- 1 can (8 ounces) tomato sauce, no sugar added (if needed)
- ¼ cup chopped fresh basil
- ¼ cup chopped fresh oregano
- 3 cups hot cooked barley (if desired)

Preparation

In a large, nonstick stockpot, combine stew meat, onion and garlic. Add olive oil and cook, stirring frequently, until buffalo meat is well browned and onion is translucent, being careful not to burn the garlic.

Add the tomatoes, tomato paste, stock, beans, dried basil, salt, Italian seasoning blend and pepper.

Bring to a boil; reduce heat and simmer, uncovered, for 30 to 45 minutes, until buffalo meat has cooked through (145 degrees) and is no longer pink and flavors have blended.

If the sauce begins to dry out during cooking, add the can of tomato sauce and continue cooking.

Stir in the fresh basil and oregano just before serving; serve over hot cooked barley if desired.

Steak with Oven-Roasted Vegetables

Satisfying enough for even the heartiest appetites, this combination of classic pan-fried steaks and deliciously charred roasted vegetables is a complete Phase Three dinner. If you would like to add an optional grain serving, try herbed wild or brown rice!

Serves: 4

Ingredients

- 1 large red onion, thickly sliced and separated into rings
- 3 medium zucchini, thickly sliced
- 3 medium yellow summer squash, thickly sliced
- 2 sweet bell peppers, any color, seeded and sliced into thick strips
- 5 cloves garlic, minced
- 1 tablespoon chopped fresh oregano
- ¼ cup chopped fresh rosemary
- ¼ cup chopped fresh basil
- ¼ cup chopped fresh parsley
- 4 lean steak filets, beef or buffalo, approximately 4 to 6 ounces each
- Sea salt and freshly cracked black pepper
- 1 to 2 plus ½ cup tablespoons organic, extra-virgin olive oil, *divided*

Preparation

Preheat oven to 400 degrees. On a large, rimmed baking sheet, toss onion, zucchini, summer squash, peppers, garlic, oregano, rosemary, basil and parsley with ½ cup olive oil, stirring well to coat evenly.

Roast the vegetables for 8 to 15 minutes, stirring frequently, until tender and edges just begin to char.

In the meantime, season steaks generously with salt and pepper.

In a large, nonstick skillet over medium heat, pan-fry in olive oil approximately 6 to 12 minutes, turning once (cooking times vary widely depending on the thickness of your steaks), until cooked to desired doneness (at least 145 degrees).

To serve, plate each steak alongside a portion of roasted vegetables and, if desired, herbed rice.

Phase Three Snacks

Fresh Vegetables with Garlic Hummus

Ingredients

- ¼ cup garlic-flavored hummus (if you can't find an all-natural garlic-flavored version, finely mince a clove of garlic and combine with plain hummus)
- 1 cup fresh vegetables (carrots, celery, tomatoes)

Preparation

Pack separately in a resealable lunch container and keep refrigerated until serving.

Crab Salad To-Go

Ingredients

- ¼ cup lump crab meat
- 1 tablespoon safflower mayonnaise
- 1 teaspoon chives

Preparation

Combine all ingredients; pack in a resealable lunch container and keep refrigerated until serving.

Celery with Almond Butter and Coconut

Ingredients

- 1 cup 2-inch celery sticks
- ¼ cup raw almond butter (prepared with approved oils)
- 1 tablespoon unsweetened shredded coconut

Preparation

Pack separately in a resealable lunch container and keep refrigerated until serving. To serve, use almond butter as a spread or a dip; sprinkle with shredded coconut.

Crisped Deli Meats with Avocado

Ingredients

- 3 slices nitrate-free deli meat (chicken, turkey or beef)
- 1 teaspoon olive oil
- ½ cup chopped avocado
- 1 teaspoon minced garlic
- 1 teaspoon lime juice

Preparation

Preheat oven to 400 degrees; lightly grease a baking sheet with olive oil. Place deli meat onto prepared baking sheet and bake for approximately 5 to 7 minutes or until browned and crisped but still flexible.

In a small bowl, mash avocado with garlic and lemon juice. Roll up deli meat slices and dip into avocado mixture.

Chapter 4

Additional

Resources

More Goodness

Other Popular Best Selling Cookbooks For Digital and Print

We have listed both the short titles and the full titles of these books to make them easier to locate.

You can also search for "best selling cookbooks 2012" or "best selling cookbooks 2013" for an up to date listing.

Other Titles by New Health CookBooks

My Virgin Diet CookBook: The Gluten-Free, Soy-Free, Egg-Free, Dairy-Free, Peanut-Free, Corn-Free and Sugar-Free Cookbook by Rebecca Lorraine

Fat Chance CookBook: The Low Sugar High Fiber Cookbook – 40 Delicious & Healthy Recipes That Your Family Will Love by New Health CookBooks

It Starts With Food CookBook: The Low Sugar Gluten-Free & Whole Food CookBook - 40 Delicious & Healthy Recipes Your Family Will Love by New Health Cookbooks

Cookbooks by Other Authors

The Fast Metabolism Diet Cookbook by Haylie Pomroy

The Fast Metabolism Diet Cookbook: Eat Even More Food and Lose Even More Weight by Haylie Pomroy

Cooking Light Cookbook by Cooking Light

Cooking Light The Essential Dinner Tonight Cookbook: Over 350 Delicious, Easy, and Healthy Meals by Cooking Light

Forks Over Knives Cookbook by Del Sroufe

Forks Over Knives-The Cookbook: Over 300 Recipes for Plant-Based Eating All Through the Year by Del Sroufe

The Low Blood Sugar Cookbook by Patricia Krimmel, Edward Krimmel

The Low Blood Sugar Cookbook: Sugarless Cooking for Everyone by Patricia Krimmel, Edward Krimmel

The Blood Sugar Solution Cookbook by Mark Hyman

The Blood Sugar Solution Cookbook: More than 175 Ultra-Tasty Recipes for Total Health and Weight Loss by Mark Hyman

Eat What You Love by Marlene Koch

Eat What You Love: More than 300 Incredible Recipes Low in Sugar, Fat, and Calories by Marlene Koch

From Mama's Table to Mine by Bobby Deen

From Mama's Table to Mine: Everybody's Favorite Comfort Foods at 350 Calories or Less by Bobby Deen

Gather, the Art of Paleo Entertaining by Bill Staley and Hayley Mason

It's All Good by Gwyneth Paltrow

It's All Good: Delicious, Easy Recipes That Will Make You Look Good and Feel Great by Gwyneth Paltrow

Jumpstart to Skinny: The Simple 3-Week Plan for Supercharged Weight Loss by Bob Harper and Greg Critser

My Beef with Meat by Rip Esselstyn

My Beef with Meat: The Healthiest Argument for Eating a Plant-Strong Diet--Plus 140 New Engine 2 Recipes by Rip Esselstyn

Nourishing Traditions by Sally Fallon

Nourishing Traditions: The Cookbook that Challenges Politically Correct Nutrition and the Diet Dictocrats by Sally Fallon

Practical Paleo by Diane Sanfilippo

Practical Paleo: A Customized Approach to Health and a Whole-Foods Lifestyle by Diane Sanfilippo

Primal Blueprint Quick and Easy Meals by Mark Sisson and Jennifer Meier

Primal Blueprint Quick and Easy Meals: Delicious, Primal-approved meals you can make in under 30 minutes by Mark Sisson and Jennifer Meier

Relish by Daphne Oz

Relish: An Adventure in Food, Style, and Everyday Fun by Daphne Oz

Superfood Smoothies by Julie Morris

Superfood Smoothies: 100 Delicious, Energizing & Nutrient-dense Recipes by Julie Morris

The America's Test Kitchen Healthy Family Cookbook by America's Test Kitchen

The America's Test Kitchen Healthy Family Cookbook: A New, Healthier Way to Cook Everything from America's Most Trusted Test Kitchen by America's Test Kitchen

The Biggest Loser Cookbook by Devin Alexander and Karen Kaplan

The Biggest Loser Cookbook: More Than 125 Healthy, Delicious Recipes Adapted from NBC's Hit Show by Devin Alexander and Karen Kaplan

The Fresh 20 by Melissa Lanz

The Fresh 20: 20-Ingredient Meal Plans for Health and Happiness 5 Nights a Week by Melissa Lanz

The Mediterranean Diet Cookbook by Rockridge University Press

The Mediterranean Diet Cookbook: A Mediterranean Cookbook with 150 Healthy Mediterranean Diet Recipes by Rockridge University Press

The Paleo Diet Cookbook by Loren Cordain and Nell Stephenson

The Paleo Diet Cookbook: More Than 150 Recipes for Paleo Breakfasts, Lunches, Dinners, Snacks, and Beverages by Loren Cordain and Nell Stephenson

What's for Dinner? by Curtis Stone

What's for Dinner?: Delicious Recipes for a Busy Life by Curtis Stone

Wheat Belly Cookbook by William Davis MD

Wheat Belly Cookbook: 150 Recipes to Help You Lose the Wheat, Lose the Weight, and Find Your Path Back to Health by William Davis MD

Weight Loss Books And Diet Books

You can also search for "weight loss books best sellers 2012" or "weight loss best sellers 2013" for a current list.

The Atkins Diet

Dr. Atkins' New Diet Revolution by Robert C. Atkins

Cooked by Michael Pollan

Cooked: A Natural History of Transformation by Michael Pollan

Eat to Live by Joel Fuhrman

Eat to Live: The Amazing Nutrient-Rich Program for Fast and Sustained Weight Loss by Joel Fuhrman

Fat Chance by Robert H. Lustig

Fat Chance: Beating the Odds Against Sugar, Processed Food, Obesity, and Disease by Robert H. Lustig

Good Calories, Bad Calories by Gary Taubes

The Blood Sugar Solution by Mark Hyman

The Blood Sugar Solution: The UltraHealthy Program for Losing Weight, Preventing Disease, and Feeling Great Now! by Mark Hyman

The 5:2 Diet Book by Kate Harrison

The 5:2 Diet Book: Feast for 5 Days a Week and Fast for 2 to Lose Weight, Boost Your Brain and Transform Your Health by Kate Harrison

The Five Two Diet Book

The Art and Science of Low Carbohydrate Living by Stephen Phinney and Jeff Volek

The Art and Science of Low Carbohydrate Living: An Expert Guide to Making the Life-Saving Benefits of

Carbohydrate Restriction Sustainable and Enjoyable by Stephen Phinney, Jeff Volek

The Fast Diet by Michael Mosley and Mimi Spencer

The Fast Diet: Lose Weight, Stay Healthy, and Live Longer with the Simple Secret of Intermittent Fasting by Michael Mosley and Mimi Spencer

The Fast Metabolism Diet by Haylie Pomroy

The Fast Metabolism Diet: Eat More Food and Lose More Weight by Haylie Pomroy

The New Atkins for a New You by Dr. Eric C. Westman, Dr. Stephen D. Phinney, Jeff S. Volek

The Paleo Solution by Robb Wolf

The Paleo Solution: The Original Human Diet by Robb Wolf, or Rob Wolf
Wheat Belly by William Davis MD

Wheat Belly: Lose the Wheat, Lose the Weight, and Find Your Path Back To Health by William Davis MD

The Primal Blueprint by Mark Sisson

The Primal Blueprint: Reprogram your genes for effortless weight loss, vibrant health and boundless energy by Mark Sisson

The Healthy Green Drink Diet by Jason Manheim

The Healthy Green Drink Diet: Advice and Recipes to Energize, Alkalize, Lose Weight, and Feel Great by Jason Manheim

Forks Over Knives by Gene Stone

Forks Over Knives: The Plant-Based Way to Health by Gene Stone

Deadly Harvest by Geoff Bond

Deadly Harvest: The Intimate Relationship Between Our Heath and Our Food by Geoff Bond

The Rosedale Diet by Ron Rosedale and Carol Colman

Ignore the awkward by Uffe Ravnskov

Ignore the awkward! How the cholesterol myths are kept alive by Uffe Ravnskov

Primal Body, Primal Mind by Nora Gedgaudas

Primal Body, Primal Mind: Beyond the Paleo Diet for Total Health and a Longer Life by Nora T. Gedgaudas, CNS, CNT

Deep Nutrition by Catherine Shanahan

Deep Nutrition: Why Your Genes Need Traditional Food by Catherine Shanahan MD

The Skinny Rules by Bob Harper

The Skinny Rules: The Simple, Nonnegotiable Principles for Getting to Thin by Bob Harper

Protein Power by Dr. Eades

Protein Power: The High-Protein/Low-Carbohydrate Way to Lose Weight, Feel Fit, and Boost Your Health--in Just Weeks! by Michael R. Eades, Mary Dan Eades

Eat to Live by Dr. Joel Fuhrman

Eat to Live: The Amazing Nutrient-Rich Program for Fast and Sustained Weight Loss by Joel Fuhrman

The Paleo Answer by Loren Cordain

The Paleo Answer: 7 Days to Lose Weight, Feel Great, Stay Young by Loren Cordain

The Seventeen Day Diet by Mike Moreno

The 17 Day Diet by Mike Moreno

The China Study by T. Colin Campbell

The China Study: The Most Comprehensive Study of Nutrition Ever Conducted And the Startling Implications for Diet by T. Colin Campbell

Choose to Lose by Chris Powell

Choose to Lose: The 7-Day Carb Cycle Solution by Chris Powell

Fit2Fat2Fit by Drew Manning

Fit2Fat2Fit: The Unexpected Lessons from Gaining and Losing 75 lbs on Purpose by Drew Manning

The Belly Fat Diet by John Chatham

The Belly Fat Diet: Lose Your Belly, Shed Excess Weight, Improve Health by John Chatham

The Dukan Diet Book by Pierre Dukan

The Dukan Diet: 2 Steps to Lose the Weight, 2 Steps to Keep It Off Forever by Pierre Dukan

The Mayo Clinic Diet Book

The Mayo Clinic Diet: Eat Well, Enjoy Life, Lose Weight by Mayo Clinic

The Mayo Clinic Diabetes Diet by Mayo Clinic

The Virgin Diet by JJ Virgin

The Virgin Diet: Drop 7 Foods, Lose 7 Pounds, Just 7 Days by JJ Virgin

101 Best Foods to Boost Your Metabolism by Metabolic-Calculator.com

Pure Fat Burning Fuel by Isabel De Los Rios

Pure Fat Burning Fuel: Follow This Simple, Heart Healthy Path To Total Fat Loss by Isabel De Los Rios

It Starts with Food by Melissa Hartwig

It Starts with Food: Discover the Whole30 and Change Your Life in Unexpected Ways by Melissa Hartwig

Shred by Ian K. Smith

Shred: The Revolutionary Diet: 6 Weeks 4 Inches 2 Sizes by Ian K. Smith

The Four Hour Body by Timothy Ferriss

The 4-Hour Body: The Secrets and Science of Rapid Body Transformation by Timothy Ferriss

VB6 by Mark Bittman

VB6: Eat Vegan Before 6:00 to Lose Weight and Restore Your Health . . . for Good by Mark Bittman

VB6: Eat Vegan Before 6:00 to Lose Weight and Restore Your Health . . . for Good by Mark Bittman

Wheat Belly by William Davis MD

Wheat Belly: Lose the Wheat, Lose the Weight, and Find Your Path Back To Health by William Davis MD

Why We Get Fat by Gary Taubes

Why We Get Fat: And What to Do About It by Gary Taubes

Made in the USA
Lexington, KY
07 February 2014